D0887305

Betrayed Broken Defiled

To order additional copies, please contact us.
BookSurge, LLC
www.booksurge.com
1-866-308-6235
orders@booksurge.com

PATTI
THEISEN

BETRAYED
BROKEN
DEFILED

The Story of A Good Life After
Abuse

2006

Betrayed Broken Defiled

ACKNOWLEDGEMENTS

My niece, Brenda Theisen Zabal, told me that something I said to her affected her very powerfully. She told me to write it down to use in my book. What book? I wasn't writing a book. I just went on my way and really didn't think about it anymore. Then a couple of weeks later, my sister Sharon Herring in Indianapolis, told me that I was going to write a book. A few weeks more passed, and a dear friend Pastor Doris Sam, also from Indianapolis, told me the same thing. Now there were three prophetic words over my life. I went into prayer and sought the Lord for a word from Him. I told Him that I had never written a book and that I could NOT write a book. The Lord told me that none of the men that had written the Bible were writers either. He told me that the Holy Spirit would inspire me and that I was to just write. I asked Him what the book would be called. When I awakened the next morning I knew the title. It would be centered on the Father, the Son, and the Holy Spirit. All knew about being "Betrayed, Broken and Defiled." Man, body, soul and spirit, all knowing betrayal, brokenness and defilement. Thus a book was born. My husband, David, was such a support to me. His love for me and his confidence in me was an inspiration in itself. And I need to acknowledge my dear sisters in the Lord, Nancy Jones and Carol Manzo, and my dear Delila Smith who encouraged me with advice, suggestions and prayers. I also need to acknowledge BookSurge

LLC, an Amazon.com company for publishing this book, and two of my dearest friends, Brian Gruss and Alana Green, for their love, support and expertise in getting this book out to the public. I also need to acknowledge the one most Betrayed, Broken and Defiled, my precious Lord and Savior, Jesus Christ. To God be the Glory.

INTRODUCTION

If you have opened this book out of some kind of curiosity and you have never known the utter betrayal, brokenness and defilement as a child at the hands of an adult, or have never been raped or otherwise demeaned and abused by a spouse or stranger, family member or close friend, or simply a date, then this book is not for you, but it may help you understand the true evil that preys on so many lives in this world.

I have actually had people tell me that any child that has been molested has in some way "asked for it." I have heard it said that children are seductive by nature and that it is society's responsibility to control their sinful urges. It is said that if a woman dresses up to look nice for her date, then she is sending a seductive message. Even a rapist or pedophile knows how ridiculous those statements are, as they thrive on the fear and domination and humiliation of their prey.

For those of you that have known firsthand what it is to lie beneath an adult while they perform their perversion atop you, or have prayed that death would overtake you so that your violation would stop, this book is for and dedicated to you. I hope that you will come to know that you can turn your *betrayed, broken and defiled* life around. Realize that there are those who understand and care and that there is hope for regaining the life you think you can only dream of. Your violation has made you, in your mind, soiled and therefore set apart from the everyday life that goes on about you. This is a lie from the very pits of hell!

What has happened is not your fault. You were in no way responsible. You never did anything wrong to bring this into your life. The purpose of this book is to restore you as a *human being*. If you are a boy or man, it is to restore your gender identity. To give you back your very soul. To bring you back into the world that you feel you are just living on the very fringes of. You are a wonderful human being and you deserve all that life has to offer.

You have asked, perhaps in rage with fists raised toward heaven, "God, why did you allow this to happen to me?" I know that I did. I blamed what I was raised to believe in, a kind, loving, and ever-present God, for totally abandoning me as a helpless child and turning me over to the adult that raped my very soul. How could this wonderful God allow this to happen to me?

I ask that you always keep in mind as you journey with me through this book that I am one of you. I will forever carry the scar of abuse. But notice that I have said *scar*. A scar represents a healed wound. It was not an easy heal. It kept breaking open and bleeding again and again. But I finally did hear from the God that I thought could not possibly have been there for me, and it was with His help that I now carry a scar and not an open wound. I thank God for my total restoration of mind, body and spirit. I am no longer consumed with hate for the person that did this to me, nor with God. Hate only consumes the hater, and we all have enough problems to deal with in everyday life. I am not saying for one minute that your rage and hatred is not totally justified. What I am saying is that it will consume every part of you if you allow it to continue. It will keep your abuse ever present. Life itself can be a constant reminder. A song, a smell, someone's cologne, a sound, can bring that abuse back into stinging reality, making you relive the incident all over again in a nanosecond.

I in no way ever want you to think that I feel I am now above the others that have been abused. When you carry a scar, damage has been done and it will never be forgotten. I just got tired of feeling that I was the gum on the bottom of the shoe of the world. Something had to give, and it was not going to be me any longer. I felt that I had to do anything to prove myself worthy, and I would do anything to be loved. My perception of what love is and how it works had become warped and distorted by my abuse.

Others prey on this lack of self-confidence, self worth and self esteem. They are small and weak cowards that depend on your "lack" to feed and protect them. You are not the gum on the bottom of someone's shoe. You are not even the shoe. You get up in the morning and slip into your shoes and go out into the world with your head held high. You do not continue to live in an abusive situation. You no longer report to your street corner and give your body and money to those who continue to prey off you. Some of you are here, and others have become bitter and reclusive and have never known a true and loving relationship. Others appear to be the life of the party but have no life of their own. And sadly, some become abusers and carry on this malignant lifestyle.

I feel such a responsibility for asking you to listen to what I have to tell you. I ask you to read this book through to the end. Please keep in mind that when you are physically wounded, you become subject to infection. You must clean the wound and apply antiseptic. Antiseptic, although it is the very thing needed to save you, can be very painful. But it is something you need to go through *to get through.*

It has taken me years to get through this ordeal. I was violated at the age of nine, and I am now fifty-seven years old. Way too much of my life was led and directed by my violation and a very emotional response to it. Emotions are spur of the moment and can lead you from one bad situation to another if you don't learn to control them. Anger was a constant companion of mine. It was quicksilver in its speed and razor sharp as I cut many good people and God out of my life. Therapy can only help you deal with your own mind. You know, more than anyone, that your very soul has been ***betrayed, broken and defiled***. I hope that I can help to restore what was taken from you and allow you to go forward and live, not as a victim, but as a survivor. A survivor is someone to be proud of. All heroes are survivors. I want you to live your life to its fullest, in spite of the person or persons that caused you such damage. So sit up. Dust yourself off. Dry your tears. Take a deep breath and let me try to give you "you" back and reintroduce you to your Creator. I want you to start loving again. And to love again, you must first start to love yourself. So come, take the hand of someone just like you, and let's get started.

CHAPTER 1
My Story

I cannot tell you how long it has taken me to write this first line. I know that the only way I can begin to help you is to let you know what happened to me. I do not want this to be ugly and graphic. To those of you who have been in this place, you can fill in your own nightmares here. But it wasn't until I was inspired to write this book that I realized just how far I really had come.

Recently I had the opportunity to pass by Fort Carson, Colorado. Quite a bit, but definitely not all, of my molestation occurred while my father was stationed at the Army base there. Yes, it was my father that molested me for years. I was adopted at birth. At about age four my mother told me how special I was and how much they wanted a little girl like me. For a few years I felt very special. When I drove past the base, a sense of overwhelming panic, sorrow and revulsion came over me. I was amazed by its intensity! Tears began to stream down my face, and I thought for a moment that I was going to be sick. I used to stand at my bedroom window and look out at Cheyenne Mountain across from the base. I would dream of running up into that mountain and hiding forever. As I said, everyday things can bring past events back into stark reality. The sight of that mountain had this power.

But as quickly as it came, this feeling passed. I realized then that I had revisited the most horrific and repulsive emotions I had ever known. I also knew that it was good for me to remember them in order to do justice to this book and to those of you I hope to help. For many of you are still dealing with the open wound and the pain, the depth of which only the abused, the betrayed, broken and defiled, can really know.

I, as many of you, once loved and trusted my abuser. I know that everyone's story is different, and it may have not been a parent or family member that hurt you, but for now, I must start at the beginning for me, and that was at the hands of my father.

Looking back, I loved to climb into my daddy's lap. He would read to me or tell me stories, or I would just settle down from my busy day and fall asleep on his lap and wake the next morning in bed. My dad was away quite a bit when I was young. The Army kept him traveling a lot. So when he did come home I was thrilled. I remember once keeping a loose tooth from falling out by holding my tongue against it so my dad could pull it when he came home. My mom and grandpa wanted to pull that tooth, but I would have no part of that. My dad was my hero, as all good dads should be for any of their children, male or female. Only my hero could pull that tooth.

Then it all changed. What had I done? Why was he angry? Why did he hurt me? Why, when I would look at him, frightened and with all the sincerity I could muster up and say, "Please, daddy, no. I don't like it," could he look at me with those dead eyes and threaten to slap me and tell me that if I didn't he wouldn't love me anymore? Nothing would ever be the same.

I have memories of parties going on downstairs while my father bent me over the bathroom sink behind a locked door as he relieved himself with me and then ordered me to "clean myself up" so there would be no evidence of his debauchery to be found by my mother. Then he would return to the party as if nothing had happened. What is worse, I would have to return to the party as well and pretend that I was just a happy, carefree ten-year-old.

I never felt safe anywhere. I never knew when the next attack would come. The worse time was when my mother was hospitalized for two weeks. The abuse was nightly, and he had nothing but time and nothing to fear. At age nine, I learned about a man's anatomy, his secretions, sexual "positions" and passionate kissing. When he was finished I was ordered, as always, to go and clean up. Part of this ritual for me was to vomit. The first night after I had dutifully cleaned up, I returned to his bed as I had been ordered to do. As I got into his bed, he told me that he didn't want me in his bed. He said it as if I should have known. He told me to go back to my own bed where I belonged. Even as a child I had the sense to say to myself, "Well, if that is where I belong, why did you make me come in here?" But he made me feel like the intruder, the one who had done something wrong, the one that was at fault for the entire evening's vile occurrences. He made me feel like the offender. As if somehow I had violated him. This is how the offenders place the blame on their victims. And as a child, you accept this subconsciously and it sets a pattern for the rest of your life. It sets the pattern of feeling unworthy of anything clean and decent.

My hatred rose to a point that I found hard to comprehend as a child. At school, with my brother and with playmates, I took charge and took no nonsense from anyone. My wrath was swift and sure. I remember my brother telling me once after I beat him up that I was crazy. Yes. That is exactly how I felt, then and for a good part of my life. I didn't know what I had done to bring this on myself, but it must have been something awful. And not being able to figure it out was driving me crazy. I could not figure out what it was, but it was MY FAULT.

The abuse continued for three more years until one day, as if someone else had taken control of my mouth, I blurted out, "If you don't stop, I'm going to tell Mom!" I thought at first that he would slap me, and I wanted to run. But much to my surprise, he laughed. He laughed! I was stunned. He said that my mother would never believe me, that she would just blame me if she even considered it at all. Now I had him. Mom wasn't like that. She was always one for doing the right thing and fairly handing out punishment for things that were bad. So I went to her. I remember the expression on her face changing as I told her. She slapped me across the face so hard that it knocked me to the floor. How dare I say such a vile and filthy thing about my father? And who had I been talking to that I could drum up such nonsense? She actually told me to "get my own man" and leave hers alone!

What? Surely I must be having a nightmare. I was not even old enough to date, and she was telling me to get my own man? I ran upstairs and passed my father in the hall. He quietly laughed at me and said, "I told you she wouldn't believe you. Now you have ruined your relationship with your mother. I hope you're happy." He was right. My mother, from that day forward, went through the motions of being the loving and perfect mother, but she showed a loathing for me in private that only changed much later in life when she needed someone to care for her. Even then, the hate would always outweigh anything that even resembled love. I grew up with two parents but in reality I had none. We looked like the typical middle class family and yet were as dysfunctional as families come.

I was asked to spend the weekend at a friend's house shortly after my mother returned from the hospital. My mother agreed.

It was my first time away from home. My first night there I got the best night's sleep I had in ages. I didn't have to half sleep and half keep my eye on the door. Not that keeping an eye on the door was going to prevent anything, but I became hyper-vigilant just the same. The second night that I was there, I got up the courage to tell my friend what my dad was doing to me. The next afternoon my girlfriend's mother came up to me in the yard, where I was playing with my little friend's brother, and slapped me very hard across the face. She informed me that I would never be allowed to come over to their house ever again and that her daughter would never be allowed to play with me ever again because I was a "filthy and evil little girl." Daddies don't do things like that to their daughters, and decent little girls do not talk about sex, ever!

I knew then that I would never be able confide in anyone. In those days, I thought that I was the only one that was going through this nightmare, and it became my "dirty" little secret. I never felt like the other kids ever again. I never belonged. Everyone was better than me.

My father stopped ejaculating in me and started ejaculating on me after my period started. My mother sat me down then and told me the facts of life. "When a man and woman fall in love," she started. LOVE?! Fall in love, and then get married, and then have sex? That wasn't the way it went. She was wrong. Then she told me that every girl is born a virgin. And she is to stay that way until she falls in love and gets married. Her virginity is a precious gift from God that is to be given only to her husband on her wedding night. I realized then that I had no gift to give anyone. I would never be married because he would know. That was as far as I could think at the age of thirteen.

It was not the last time that my mother would remind me that virginity was a special gift. Even after I told her what my father had done, she stayed in total denial. And yet she knew. I told her, so she knew. She took great pleasure in punishing me by always reminding me, with a friendly lilt to her voice, to watch myself with the boys because only "good and decent girls" could find a good man to marry them. No decent man would want someone else's discards.

To the world, she was a good mother. But her hatred was real to me. She went through all the motions of being loving and supportive. She insisted on making all my clothes by hand. Yes, they were beautiful, but she did it for herself and all those she perceived as watching her raise adopted children that she had taken an oath before a judge to raise responsibly. She would always assure me when handing over a newly made frock that I didn't deserve it because of the way I treated her and my father. It was clear that I would forever pay for the sins of my father that were somehow, still not clear to me, my fault.

I grew up angry and hateful. In my teen years I made as much trouble for my parents as I could and always showed them, in little ways that would not get me hurt, how much I hated them both. Lucky for me, I never got into any real trouble and I never got into trouble with the law. But rebellion can cause parents grief in my mind, grief they deserved and grief they got!

Later in life, as I went from one bad relationship to another, my parents would act stunned at my ability to get involved with such "losers." The pain deepened and the self-loathing grew. I just got to the point where I wanted to die.

I married at nineteen to someone who was not looking for a virgin but a good time girl. I was fine with the sex and plenty of it before we were married. But once we married and it was expected of me, once he started his position as "man of the house" taking charge of things, I came to distrust him just as I did my father. To me he became my father and I grew to hate him. I knew then that I was not able to love anyone. Even myself. I had two children, one right after another, and divorced. I raised my boys by myself, again going from one failed relationship to another. What I didn't realize at the time is that I was teaching my boys a very unhealthy and unstable lifestyle.

I continued the act of belonging to a good family. I went with my boys to family functions. Holiday parties, reunions, days spent up at the cottage on the lake in Wisconsin. All seemed so normal. Well, except for, as the extended family members would whisper, my "many strange relationships." I could not be involved in a "normal" relationship. I, if I took anyone along at all, never took the same person to any family function. As soon as someone started thinking of me in terms of love and a relationship with some kind of commitment, it meant that that man would control me somehow and I would "have" to have sex with him when it wasn't my idea. The moment I got to the point where I was not in control, I was gone. I never made love to anyone. I had sex. I mean, you had to have sex in order for someone, anyone, to love you right? Inside I was dying for love and affection. But because it had been planted in my mind that "let me have sex with you then I will love you," I was always on the road to further destruction in my life. When I was first molested, my father had put that thought deep in my soul. "If you don't let me, I won't love you."

My life became a series of affairs with men who were single and married. I liked the married men best because there would be no possibility of commitment and having to do anything for them or with them that did not have my approval. I was in control. I am talking about this now as if I really knew what was going on then. I was a total mess and out of control. At the time I was responding subconsciously to what had happened to me. I never, thank God, got involved with drugs. I had so many violent reactions to prescription medications as a child that I was terrified of any drugs. But now, alcohol, there was a true friend. It always numbed me to the point that I was convinced that I actually loved my life and that everything was "normal."

I am trying to put what I did in some sort of perspective from where I stand now, looking back at my life. And I would imagine that those of you who have gone through abuse are shaking your heads, knowing that your behavior was or is almost the same. Sadly, unless you do something, it will continue this way until the day you die. It will rob you of everything good life has to offer, a healthy lifestyle, and most of all, self respect and love. If you cannot love yourself, you cannot love anyone else, including your children, in the way that they deserve.

At the age of twenty-nine I took an overdose of Valium that I had stolen from my girlfriend's medicine cabinet. Surely, with my low tolerance to drugs, this would do the trick. I did not realize then that I would have gone to hell for my efforts. That would have been an eternal mistake. I woke up in the hospital with a tube in my nose that went down my throat. I tried to look around, but my eyes would barely move. Great! I had been a failure at this too. Apparently, judging by my inability to move my eyes I was now going to be a vegetable. Then the reality of what I had done set in. Where were my kids? Why had I done this? Now I would lose the only good thing in my life, my boys. Even though I never let those kids get close to me either, I loved them dearly.

It is funny how you can continue the "sins of the father" so to speak. Abused people can become abusers too. Some actually do the same abuse as they suffered..-I, thankfully, have never been able to understand this syndrome. Some become just as distant from their children as they do any other relationship in their lives. I fell into this category. Yes, I loved my boys, but I never gave them a secure, stable home environment. Nor did I provide them with a nurturing relationship; time spent holding them in my lap and cuddling. I always put me first and just carried them along for the ride. I was very stern with them. I was never a "huggie touchy" mom. They would love to come into my room on a Saturday morning and get into bed with me to watch cartoons. I would get out and sit on top of the covers to watch TV with them. I quit giving them baths at the age of about four. I just told them how to bathe and ran down the list of parts that should be clean by the time they were out of the tub. I could never cuddle my kids. To be honest, it made me so uncomfortable it would almost make me physically ill. I just never wanted my kids to feel the revulsion I felt from any bodily contact with my dad. Not even a hug from my dad was tolerable.

I never feared my father hurting my boys. After all, they were BOYS! Guys like girls, right? .When I was a girl, the word "gay" meant that you were really happy and care free. No one talked openly about homosexuality or pedophilia for that matter. It just was not in my mind-set even when my children were young. I truly never gave one moment's thought as to the safety of my boys when it came to their spending time with my parents. My parents would take my boys on vacation with them for a couple of weeks at a time. I should have been very concerned. Both my boys were molested by my father. Later I found out from my brother that he, too, was abused by my father!

The guilt for not protecting my boys almost drove me insane! My father had ruined so many lives. This vile behavior has to be stopped! All of us have to stop it. It is a plague, as deadly as any pandemic known to man! I, for the first time, understood the rage that provokes some people to end the life of another. I am not sure what I would have done had my father still been alive. My mother was still alive. She would hear about abuse on talk shows and would *tisk, tisk* the television: "Those people are degenerates and should be shot." The thing that amazed me most was the day that she actually said that she was so glad that she and my father had seen to mine and my brother's safety from things like that. She said that it was the reason that they were so strict and made sure that they knew where we kids were at all times.

I realized then that there was something wrong with her mind. My father was a womanizer. He cheated on my mom continuously. He would be totally inappropriate right in front of her and in front of us kids. She would sometimes confide in me later as to what had made her so angry. A twelve-year-old child is not someone to whom a mother should confide things of this nature. Why should these things make her any more angry than what I told her my father was doing to me? My mother was an extremely light sleeper. So I knew as a kid that when my dad was out, and my mom would fall asleep on the couch and he would come home and come upstairs into my bedroom, she had just *let* him. Was she that afraid of losing him? Did she think that it was better for him to use me at home, and that way she knew where he was at least? It was odd that once he went downstairs as quietly as he had come upstairs, she would wake up right away. Looking back now, I see that my mother was a very sick individual in her own right. I wonder what happened in her life to cause her problems. Life is very hostile, and if we don't take control of our lives, the nightmares of the world just continue.

Once, as a girl scout, I went to a home for the elderly at Christmas time. We served cookies and sang Christmas carols. The place stank, and the patients all looked like zombies to me. The people taking care of them seemed cold and mean, and no one was even a little happy. I vowed, even though my home life was a nightmare, that I would never allow anyone I knew go into a place like that.

Well, be careful what you wish for, as they say. I went home and told my parents about the terrible time I had and that I would never see them in a place like that. That little statement from my heart, even though it had been violated and broken, is what God would use later in my life. The time came when my father became very ill and had to have bypass surgery. He would recover and fail and recover again until it just got to the point that my mother could not take care of him. Of all that had transpired in our lives, the only thing at this point that stood out in their minds was my promise all those years ago. I had also promised myself long ago that no matter what, I would never become like them. I was going to try to do the best for everyone to the best of my ability, no matter what they had done to me. Well, I had my parents move in with me. They sold their home in Florida and moved to Indiana to live with me. My father died in my home in a comfortable room with nurses that would come to the house to check him. My mother and I saw to feeding him. After his ability to make it to the bathroom failed, my mother would change him and I would do his laundry. I learned that you cannot always depend on Depends!!

I went into my father's room one evening just before he died. I told him to remember that I forgave him for everything that he had done when I turned my life over to God, and that all I wanted from him was for him to tell me that he was sorry for what he had done to me. That old man gritted his teeth and turned his face and looked out the window. I just stood there for a couple of moments and then became aware that he was not going to do it. So I told him that it didn't matter. That at this point, whether or not he was sorry was between him and God. I did not need his apology. I told him to quit fighting so hard. I told him that he was to seek Jesus. To reach out to Him and say he was sorry, and God would take him home. I don't know if my father ever did this. But at the end, when he was not able to turn over by himself, he was lying on his back the last time I looked in on him. In the morning when we found him dead, he was on his side and his hand was stretched out as if taking someone else's hand.

My father never stopped tormenting me even after he physically stopped molesting me at the age of fourteen when I told him that I would kill myself. It worked; he stopped, but he was always asking if he could be with me. He always reminded me that I was adopted and not really his daughter so it never had been or would be wrong. Every time I thought that he had reached the limit of his vileness, he would surprise me. I realized then that he did not love me as a father, nor had he ever done so.

When I was fourteen, my father went into teaching ROTC at a nearby university even though he remained in the Army until I was seventeen. We moved to a normal city, not an Army base, and I started dating the next year. My father would drill the boys who came to pick me up. He always implied that they were taking me out just for sex. Couldn't anyone take me out just because they liked me and enjoyed my company? Was it always about sex? How I hated him.

At this point I just stopped caring about anything, especially myself. I remember once that I went out with a guy to the drive-in. He had bought a 7UP at the snack bar, and when he got back into the car he put the drink on the dashboard and it fell into my lap. I was soaked. When I got home I started to go right upstairs because I was a sticky, uncomfortable mess. My father went into a rage. The back of my pant suit was dirty. I had apparently acted like a sponge with my wet pants. My date's seats were less than clean but they must have been spotless after I slid across them. Anyway, my dad went to dust the back of my pants off and when he felt they were wet he started slapping me in the face and told my mother to take me upstairs and "check me." My mother asked me what had happened, and I told her. She told me to go to bed, but it was *always* about sex with him.

Oddly enough, forty years later, I am now married to one of the boys my father drilled. He said that my dad gave him the creeps when he would come over to the house to pick me up. He said my dad would look at him with this smirk on his face like he knew my future husband was going to get laid. Everyone I knew thought my dad was weird. *Weird* was not the word for it. The hypocrisy was the hardest to live with. Father would tell me to make the boys respect me. Oh! Strangers should be made to respect me? How about you, Father? Who will make *you* respect me?

I had fallen in love with the boy I am now married to. He was always such a gentleman with me. He never tried anything. But one night during a date, I told him to take me home. He was shocked. I told him I was sick and needed to go home. He tried to change my mind, but took me home anyway. You see, I thought the world of this boy and I knew that he was very fond of me. What if things progressed? What if we both fell in love? What if he asked me to marry him? My mother told me all those years ago and continually reminded me during my teen years while dating that a man knows if a woman is a virgin or not on their wedding night. How could I look into the eyes of this wonderful guy and see loathing? I had to get away. Someone wonderful like that should not be with someone as filthy as me. He never asked me out again. My life was a mess then and would continue for that way for over three decades.

Remember that I mentioned that drinking had become my friend? Well, by the time I was in my thirties it was pretty bad. I had managed to keep it from my boys; I always came home late and they never saw me. But by the time I was in my thirties they were in their early teens, and they began to see me in a different light. I began to feel totally inadequate as a mother. How did such wonderful kids get stuck with a mother like me? I didn't even feel worthy of my own kids. I didn't drive a minivan. I didn't sit in the stands with a respectable man by my side as my boys played ball. I stopped going to their games because it seemed to point out to me even further what a loser I was. And as much as I dreamed of settling down with a wonderful, decent man that would be a good father figure to my boys, the thought of the control that man would have over me made it impossible to consider. I always dated weak men who either had to depend on me or were easily manipulated. I ended up hating these poor guys for reasons they never understood. I used a lot of people in my life and then just tossed them aside, just like my dad used me and tossed me aside. What a sick pattern had developed in my life. As much as I had tried to never be like my parents, I actually was in many ways.

One night I came home so drunk that I could not even

remember how I made it home. I remember that the boys were laughing, but there was a strange look on their faces. It was fear. The last thing I remember is the boys helping me onto the bed. Apparently I had passed out into my closet. The next morning I was sicker than I had ever been after a night of drinking. Later I would find out from friends that I had downed thirteen vodka martinis. How I didn't die was a miracle.

Thoughts of suicide came to me again. I wasn't any good to anyone and never would be. Why was my life like this? Why did other people live such wonderful and fulfilling lives? What was wrong with me? I finally raised my fists into God's face and asked Him "Why?" Was He even really there? I had gone to Catholic school most of my life and always heard of this loving and wonderful God. I sat next to my parents in church every Sunday without fail, watching people bow their heads and worship God. Even my father bowed his head and prayed after abusing me the night before. I was always amazed that if God was the way that I was taught he was toward sinners, why my dad did not burst into flames by merely walking into the church! How could God just stand by and watch me as a child being molested by my father? How could He stand by and allow women and men and innocent children to be raped and brutalized? How could He just allow all the ills of this world to continue and expect people to love Him? Maybe there was no God, and I was not in His face at all but merely screaming at the ceiling.

CHAPTER 2
Something Strange Happens

I knew after that drunken night that something had to happen. I was either going to kill myself, or get help. It was four o'clock in the morning. I had awakened to go to the bathroom to be sick. I had never been that drunk or sick before in my life. If I was going to kill myself, it sure was not going to be by drinking myself to death. That hurt too much, and the looks on my kids' faces was forever imprinted on my mind. Pills were the only way to go. It would not be hard to find some. Heck, everyone I knew was on some kind of drugs. And I knew from my previous failure that I would have to take twice as many to do the job right. My boys would be much better off without me. I would leave a letter asking that they go to my brother to raise.

Now fasten your seatbelt, because this is where the real bumpy ride starts.

I turned on the television as I got into bed after another night of partying late. I thanked the God that wasn't there that the next day was Sunday and that I could stay in bed and not have to go into work. Cable television was not what it is today, and basic cable gave me very little to choose from at four in the morning. Oh, lucky me. It was a televangelist. Sigh, But it was something to watch to take my mind off my stomach.

Suddenly, the televangelist spun around, pointed his finger into the camera, and yelled, "There is a woman out there watching me now who is ready to start heaving her guts out again because she is so drunk. You are so drunk that you are sitting on your bed with one leg on the floor to keep the room from spinning." I looked down at my leg that was on the floor in awe! "And you have allowed your children to see you drunk," the televangelist continued. "Worse than that, you are thinking of committing suicide." I almost screamed. Maybe I was having a nightmare. Maybe I had gone insane.

The man on the television told me that God had heard me curse Him. He said that God would help me if right now, right there in my bedroom, I would get on my face before Him and ask for His help. I threw myself down on the floor and wept like I had never wept before. "Oh, God, help me." It was then that I realized that I rarely had ever cried. But now the tears were coming to the point I could hardly breathe. In my mind I begged God to help me.

After I quit crying, it was 6:00 a.m. Now I knew that I had gone mad. Where had the past two hours gone? I must have blacked out. But wait. Something else was wrong. I was not drunk anymore. I was not sick, not even a little. And I was so hungry. What had happened to me? I wasn't just hungry for breakfast, I was hungry for God. I knew for sure that there was a God and that He wanted to help me. I got my kids up and apologized to them for allowing them to see me that way again. I told them that I was going to make some changes in my life. I also told them that after breakfast, we were going to church. Their mouths dropped open. "Church? You? Wow, Mom!" The first church we came to was a Baptist church. We went in. I didn't care what kind of church it was. (Well, it was not going to be a Catholic church) I just needed to be in church. I felt as though every eye was on me as my boys and I walked down the isle to find a seat. They all looked so, well, holy! (Let me inform you here that every pew has a story and that is why they call them "Pews") Most have testimonies that would shock you. I was sure that they knew how horrible and soiled I was. But when I really looked back at them they were smiling and saying welcome. I felt God. It felt good.

The kids and I went back that next Wednesday night. I went up to the altar and gave my life to Jesus and got down on my knees and cried as I had never cried before.. I felt all the poison start to come out. I would cry at the drop of a hat for the next three months as a sort of purging began to take place. I found myself reading the Bible, asking questions, reading anything that I could get my hands on to find out more about this God I had heard of but had never truly known on a personal level. Later, and of their own free will, my children accepted Christ as well.

Now I would love to tell you that all went well in my life. That I never reverted to my old ways and that all my relationships from that point on were beautiful. But I can't. I, like everybody, am human. The flesh is very weak. The old paths are the easiest to follow. But I did learn one thing: When I was walking the road that God pointed out, things went much better.

Somehow, though, I kept thinking that I knew better. One of the first things that I learned, and this would prove to be the hardest, is that in order for God to forgive my sins, I would have to forgive *everyone* that I had issues with! Why would God expect that of me? He knew what my parents had put me through. Forgiveness was out of the question. God would understand. I knew that He knew what had happened to me, and He would not mind if I just skipped this one little order. I went on without forgiving anyone. Oh well, so not to be completely insensitive to God, I forgave a friend of mine that had made me very angry and that I had stopped talking to. God must have been overjoyed right? I know my friend was.

Another thing that I was supposed to do was to share my salvation. Well, I didn't have to be told to, I wanted to. I was so happy. And it came to me that I had known one other person as happy as I now felt. Prior to being saved, I had hired a young girl to work for me. I almost regretted it the moment she started. I was a miserable person and loved to share my misery. But I could not make this young thing miserable. She did her job with joy in her heart and a song on her lips daily, no matter what mood I was in or how much of a workload I gave her. The one thing that she did do that enraged me was that she always spoke of being a Christian. Boy, did I have fun with that! She started singing *Amazing Grace* constantly. I finally told her that this was not a church but a place of business and that she had to stop. Well, then she started whistling it! I warned her again. You guessed it: she started humming it. I went into her office and told her that if she continued I would find some reason, any reason, to fire her. I never heard another thing out of her, but I could swear that she was tapping that song with the end of her pen on her desk. And she continued to be happy and perky until the day she left. I know now that somehow God had put this kid into my path, to plant a seed that would later grow into knowledge of Him. Although I would not admit it at the time, part of my anger towards her was because I envied her joy. Nothing upset her. She would say that she could do all things through Christ that strengthened her.

I called her and gave her my good news. She didn't believe me. She thought that I had just called to make fun of her some more. I laughed and told her to call my pastor for confirmation. A couple of days later I got a call from her, and she was crying.

She said she was so happy and that she had been praying very hard that God would find a way to touch my heart. She said that she did not know what had made me so bitter and ugly, but that she knew God could fix anything. We talked and cried together after that. I thanked her over and over for her prayers. We haven't really talked since. But somehow I know she still prays for me. And I know that we will see each other again. If not here on earth, then in heaven.

I am sure that almost all of you reading this book have had a similar event happen to you. Those Christians are all over the place annoying everyone, aren't they? And you know that you are way past God having anything to do with you right? All those prim and proper folks sitting in their pews would sneer and mock you, right? Who are they anyway, to judge you? What do they know of your suffering? What do they know about standing on a street corner selling yourself and then giving all your money to some pimp who says he loves you and is the only one you can depend on? And how many of those kids are sitting in church next to someone who molested them the night before? I know your thoughts. I have been there. I have never stood on a street corner and sold myself nor have I been beaten half to death by a husband, boyfriend or pimp. Nor am I am a boy that has been raped by another man. But I have my story, too, that you just read. And I am now one of those people that sit in the pews. I know now that almost every seat in every pew has a story to tell of how God found someone and changed their life. You don't have to go looking for God, because He is not lost. He comes to you because He knows *you* are lost. When He comes for you, don't miss the opportunity to take His hand and follow Him to complete and final salvation from everything you have been subjected to, and even eternal death. But I will tell you one thing. I have not now nor will I ever forget where I was before God found me. And there is not one day that passes that I do not pray for all of you. And if you will please just continue to turn these next pages, I will tell you of my journey to where I am now. And why I am writing this book and why I pray for all of you. Where ever you are and whomever you are. Some *ONE* person started this vicious cycle in your life that is leading to the destruction of your very soul. And believe me, your soul is something that your violators can not touch. Only you are in charge of that. Think for a minute before you decide that I am just another one of those bible thumping idiots getting in your face. I am here to tell you that there is a God and that he will punish and send to damnation *ANYONE* that turns their back on Christ and harms a child of God. You need to get yourself out from among them. I will tell you how later. You need God on your side. He does care and he does love you. How can he, knowing what you have gone through? I will get into that also. But this is where you need to make the decision to listen to the rest of my story for your soul's sake. I, at this point just might be your nagging young girl that is singing the praises of God, "Tra, lah, lah, lah, lah". But all I ask is that you hear me out. I asked God that burning question that haunts us all. *Why?* Where were you? And he answered me. The answer was there all the time. It's like Dorothy in The Wizard of OZ. She asked the good witch Glenda how to get home, and Glenda told her she (Dorothy) had the answer all along, but she had to learn it for herself because no one could tell her. And his answer shocked me and it will shock you as well. I will reveal his answer later. I guess the bottom line here is just this. Do you want to spend *ETERNITY* with the very one or ones that have hurt you?! Eternity is a very long time. And after you die you will not have a chance to rid yourselves of these people. You will be tormented by them forever. And the demons that occupy hell will make your abusers look like girl or boy scouts! I could not bear that thought. It still frightens me to just think of it and I have done something about my eternity. I don't want you to be a victim any longer let alone for eternity. So let's go on.

I continued to go to church and took my sons with me. I went to a lot of churches seeking what I and my spirit were comfortable with. It could not be anything that was even similar to the Catholic Church for me. This is not a condemnation against the Catholic Church, but it is just a reminder where I sat so many Sundays watching my dad pray. So in this sense, I guess that it is still a little bit of baggage that I carry with me. I did not need a church that was controlled by ritual but a place where my spirit could soar with the wings of an eagle.

I knew my life would change, and slowly, as I learned more, it did. I asked God why I could not have all the goodies right away. He gave me this analogy. If I were driving down the road and saw someone in trouble, such as a homeless person, and I picked this person up in their current situation and took them home to care for them, would I leave my wallet out in plain sight? Would I leave them, unsupervised, with my children? I knew the answer was no. God assured me that He loved me and was going to help me, but I had a lot of learning and growing up in Him to go through and that good things come to those willing to wait upon the Lord. I knew then that I could not go on with my life the way it was, and I needed God's help to turn things around. After all, I sought God because I hated my life so much that I was anxious to end it. What good would it be to me or my soul for things to continue the way they had been going before I gave myself to Jesus? I hated my life and God is not about hate.

I finally found a Bible-based, Spirit-filled church where

I was comfortable. Everyone must find a place to worship God that suits them. You must find a place where there is counseling and love and prayer. The important thing is to get there. Now, did I become one of those devout pew sitters right away? Well, I would for a while, and then the world would call, and I would answer. I thought so many times that I had made friends with God and that He would stand by me no matter what; so, because I thought that I could handle anything on my own, I would just do it *my* way. I would backslide and find that the world had not changed, that it was still there, willing to swallow me up. I would find myself swearing again. Then, what could it hurt if I took just one little drink? But it did hurt. It was never just one little drink. I had to keep up with the others, right? It put me right back on the path that I begged God to save me from.

So back I would go to God with my tail between my legs. Would He forgive me? Yes, of course. God cannot lie. We start each morning with a clean slate with God if we confess our sins. Would He only give me a few chances? No, He will never leave or forsake me, for He knows my heart. So for a while, I got into the habit of doing my own thing, so to speak, and then going back to God when the guilt got heavy enough. This actually went on for a good five years! God would richly bless me. And then Miss Superior here thought that she had the system down pat and could handle it from there. WRONG!

You see, there is another real entity out there in the world. He has been minimized by Hollywood. He is in every monster movie that children and adults are told is just make believe. Or perhaps you don't believe in him either. Satan is *real*. He hates everyone, even the fools that worship him and think they are getting demon brownie points for the hereafter. He is waiting every time you drift away from God. He loves your misery. It is what makes him tick. You are literally playing with him when you think that you can handle your life by yourself.

Once I finally got that into my thick head, I did not drift away from God again. Do I sin? Yes. We all do. We all sin and fall short of the glory of God. But that is why God sent another real person by the name of Jesus. How many of you would give up your child, would have them give up their life for some sin, some transgression, some broken law committed by someone else, and have them suffer the death penalty? I am sorry, but I would not be able to sacrifice one of my children for anyone, not even you. And yet, this is what God sent His only son to do for each one of us. This is huge! I never get over the depth of this act. Then imagine someone telling you that the officials know that people in the future will commit crimes, so your child must be put to death for what they will do long after he has been alive! We would think that totally insane. And yet, you and I continue to sin, and the price was already paid over 2000 years ago.

Once I got this firmly in my mind, I no longer wanted to go it on my own. People are coming forward about abuse and molestation these days. Talk shows have had many brave souls go public with their horror stories. Many actors and actresses have come forward lately. This helps. But the world is cruel, and there will always be those who have ridiculous opinions that continue to mentally harm those of us that have told our stories publicly. The courts make excuses for the behavior of these monsters who have tormented us, and many are set free again to inflict their sick agendas on an unsuspecting world. There are many Crisis Centers that will hide you from your molesters. There are doctors and psychologists by the literal thousands that will put you in therapy for years. I went through some of these channels. Nothing would give me relief. Sometimes

I would hear someone cough and it reminded me of the way that my dad coughed and I would go spiraling down into evil memories and flashbacks. This was not the answer. I had heard a phrase from the Bible that says, "Whom God sets free, is free indeed". That is the kind of freedom I was looking for. It is what I needed. Once I realized just how awesome Christ was and what he did for me, I knew I had to quit playing with my soul. *I did not want to end up spending eternity with the very person that made my life a living hell.* I had to find out more about this God. I had questions. I had a lot of questions for this God. I imagine that they are the same questions you have asked him directly or of someone else in a conversation relating to God.

I'll make a list for you and as we go on I will do my best to address each one. I will share the revelations and truths I found. All I knew is that I was at a point in my life where I was either going to go on, totally entrenched with God, or I was going to go back to the way I was. That thought scared me. I had seen changes in my life and I knew that God was responsible. The real lows came when I walked away from Him and tried it my own way again. But to go on with God, I needed answers. I needed to get these questions that separated me from God out of the way once and for all. We all have doubts. But if we will only invest a little time in "ourselves" we can get rid of the very doubts that will keep us from knowing our Creator.

Do not forget that the most heinous molester of all time is Satan himself. He does not want even one of us to get away from his torment or his tormentors. I did not want to spend eternity with him either. I knew that if I was going to defeat an invisible enemy, I needed the power of the invisible God to do it. Do not ever delude yourself into thinking you can defeat Satan on your own.

How often have you made the statement, to yourself, or to

another, that your life is a living hell? Here is great news! Christ did something about that, and we have the ability to stop the living hell in our lives. There are Christians that sit in church every Sunday who have missed this wonderful revelation. Once I realized just how wonderful Christ was I knew that I had to stop playing with my soul. I did not want to spend eternity in hell with the very person that had made my life a living hell. I needed to learn all I could about God because I realized He was all that I really had left.

CHAPTER 3
A Reintroduction to God 101

If you are there God, why do You let these terrible things happen to me?

Let's address this first and most difficult of questions, that most of us, if not all of us, have asked at some point in their lives. How does such a good God let such bad things happen? Many books have been written for, and read almost exclusively by, Christians regarding this issue. But for those not familiar with the Bible, these books with their answers merely fly over the heads of those seeking to understand. I am going to give it to you as clearly as I can. I am going to keep it as simple as I can and not end up sounding like I am talking down to you.

We all have heard of Adam and Eve unless we have been beamed here from another planet. I have personally met some people that I am sure have been beamed here! The story of Adam and Eve varies depending on how old you are when you heard it. But now that we are all grown up, we need to address the basics of what actually occurred in Eden. This is vital because it changed the world as we now know it. It was very different back then, before Adam and Eve thought that they, too, could go it alone without God. And let's not forget who else was there, sticking his evil nose into God's business. Satan was ruining lives that far back. In fact, what he did, and what Adam and Eve did in response to his temptation, put you and me and the rest of humanity into the place we find ourselves this very day.

The first thing that you must firmly get settled into your mind is that **God is perfect**. When He makes a decision or a law, it is perfect. It is perfect to the point that God Himself has to honor His own actions, decisions and Word.

None of us are capable of this perfection. Some of us set down guidelines for our own lives. But for the most part we falter and change our minds, or we alter the course if what we have laid out for ourselves becomes too tedious for us to handle. That is why resolutions such as quitting smoking or going on a diet fail. We set down a law for ourselves: "I am going to throw this pack of cigarettes out the window and I am never going to touch another one again." Well, a day later we are thinking that perhaps we were too hasty and that maybe just cutting back a little every week is a better way to go. Then a crisis occurs and we tell ourselves that no one would expect us to give up what keeps us from killing everyone at a time like this! Before you know it, we are saying that this is just not the time to stop; we will address this issue later. And let's not forget the worldwide ongoing diet!

But God is not and cannot be like this. Did you ever stop to realize that there is perfect order to the universe? I don't care how many people continue to delude themselves that there was a "Big Bang" and that everything just happened to land in the right place to support life as we know it. It is God's perfection that keeps perfect order in the universe. So when God speaks, He shows His *integrity*. Wouldn't it be nice if there were true integrity in the world? There is no perfect integrity but that of God. We all have been promised things by mortal man, but if you are honest, you have been lied to, totally deceived, or swayed to do someone's bidding. God is not like that. You can take what He says for fact and truth.

Let's go back a little further than the appearance of Adam

and Eve. When just heaven existed, all the angels were given duties, so to speak. All had their place in heaven. Even the angels had free will. Lucifer, who became Satan, was the most beautiful of all the angels. He was actually in charge of music and praise and worship of God. He became self-loving and envious of all the beautiful music and praise going to God and not to him.

Now, anyone that has a job knows that there always seems to be that one person who wants to climb to the top of the heap no matter whom they have to step on to get there. I don't care if you are in a corporate setting or work on a street corner. Someone always wants to be the boss' pet or replace the boss himself. And they can never do this alone—misery loves company and reassurance. So they start gossiping and backbiting and they get others to take their side by lying or making up lies about others. Pretty soon you have people turning on each other and life becomes "hell" to deal with in that place. (No pun intended, but what the heck?)

The same happened in heaven. Lucifer started catching other angels at the water cooler and in corners, planting seeds of doubt and rebellion in their minds. Some told him to get away, but others agreed. Those in agreement formed an army of sorts, and a full rebellion to overthrow heaven occurred. The good angels of God defeated Lucifer and his army and cast them down to earth. They were not given a new place to rule or take authority over but were sent to a lonely desolate place that separated them from God. You know, like the place you are right now. Being separate from your Creator is a lonely place. We all have someone we miss when we are away from them. Most, but yes, not all, have homesickness when we are away from those who gave birth to us and who took care of us and who showed us love. There is a natural bond, and you know when it is not there. It is such a lonely feeling isn't it?

God created you in His image and likeness, and He misses you, too. He created you to share in His creations and love. He created you to extend His love to the natural world He has created. God created you to share all He is and has made for you. You must remember the world God created, not the world that resulted when Adam and Eve gave up, turned over, and sold their rightful authority to Satan by taking his challenge and believing his lies and deception, was made for man's dominion over it. We have all, at one time or another, listened to someone else and truly regretted that decision. As a result we had to live with the circumstances created by our bad decision. The world is now the way it is as a result of Adam and Eve's bad decision.

Now, I know that we have been discussing "bad" fathers and "bad" people in general. But let's all keep in mind that there are awesome fathers out there, and let's use them to draw on as our image of what a wonderful father is like. God is the ultimate awesome Father. He provided man, His child, with a beautiful and flawless home. He created him first with a spirit so that he could communicate with God, as our father, God, who is also a Spirit, and then with a body so that he could exist and function on the physical earth, which was a beautiful garden and a restful place.

God also gave man a free will. You may wonder why God gave man free will if He already knows who will find their way back home to Him and who will not. But that is not the point. If you have ever had a child, you know that from the day that child is born your biggest line is, "Say mama, can we say mama, coochie, coochie?" So eventually the child blurts out "Mama" and this little bundle of joy makes your life complete. You entirely forget that you have practically brainwashed that child to say "Mama". But one day, out of the blue, when this child has experienced ups and downs and has learned some of life's hard lessons, this child says, fully of his own free will, "Thanks, Mom and Dad, for being there for me. I love you so much." How much more does that mean to a parent? Because this time it was said of the child's own free will. He was not coached or rehearsed. He said it just out of knowledge and love. It is the same way with God. He most certainly could have created a world of zombies that walked around all day reciting, "I love you, God, I love you, God." But what kind of fellowship would that be? If we want sincerity, then how much more does our Father want it?

When God gave earth to Adam and Eve, He instructed them to inhabit and take dominion over everything God had provided, from the earth itself to the birds, animals and creatures that were on it and under it. They could touch everything and eat anything except of the fruit of the Tree of Knowledge of Good and Evil. (There were actually two special trees in the Garden of Eden. One was the Tree of the Knowledge of Good and Evil. This was the tree they were not to eat from. The other was the Tree of Life. This tree they could eat freely from as it gave them eternal youth and life). Now, remember that I told you that Lucifer (Satan) had been cast down to earth? Sometime between God creating the heavens and earth and creating man, Satan was banished to earth. Satan knew of hate, jealousy, sin, lies and deception, and of being self-serving. These things are at the bottom of all greater sins like theft and murder and so on. Satan was here with his knowledge of these things and of his own treachery against God. He still hated God and wanted still to kill, steal, and destroy anything of God.

One day Satan, disguised as a serpent, one of God's good creations, found Eve and asked her if God really told her and

Adam not to eat of any tree in the garden. She replied that they could eat from any tree except one that was in the middle of the garden. They were not even to touch it or they would surely die. Satan assured her that they would not actually, physically die, but that God knew if they ate that fruit they would then have the knowledge of good and evil just like God himself, and God did not want that. Like I said, we have all known people who twist the truth in order to accomplish their own agenda. Well, Eve looked at the fruit and knew it was eatable, and now she wanted a taste of this knowledge that Satan talked about. So she ate and gave Adam some to eat, too. The simple eating of the fruit forever broke the relationship between God and man. Adam and Eve sold out humanity with a simple taste of forbidden fruit. They literally gave their right of dominion over the earth to Satan, who stole it with his lies. If Adam and Eve had simply told Satan that God was so good to them, if He did not want them to eat from just this one tree then it was not too much to ask, then we all would be living in the Garden of Eden to this very day.

When God came to the garden to visit with Adam and Eve as He always did, He had to call for them because they were hiding. When God saw the looks on their faces and the leaves that covered them, He asked them what they had done. There is much emphasis in the Bible about Adam and Eve's nakedness. Think of it this way. When we are very young we run all over naked as the day we were born, if we can, because of the comfort and freedom it gives us. Our parents have to tell us that outside of our home, and eventually inside it, that is not appropriate. When Adam and Eve were in the will of God in the Garden, they were not even aware that they were naked. But once they had sinned, they separated themselves from the glory of God that covered them, and for the first time they noticed their nakedness. They not only wanted to hide themselves from God but from each other. They grabbed the nearby fig leaves and tried to weave them together to cover themselves.

When God asked them what they had done and why they were covered, Adam told the first lie, and the first finger-pointing party commenced. He said that when he heard God come into the garden he hid because he was naked. Well, God had visited with them many times before, and being naked had never bothered them. God asked them how it was that they knew they were naked. He asked if they had eaten from the Tree of Knowledge of Good and Evil. Adam told God that the woman that God had seen fit to give him gave him the fruit, so he ate it. It was almost as if Adam were telling God that if He had not created Eve then none of this mess would have happened. So God asked Eve what she had done, and she was not about to take the blame either; she said the devil made her do it. God told Satan that because of what he had done, he would be cursed above all things, man and beast and that he would always crawl on his belly and eat dust for all his days.

And this is the saddest part of this story. God told Adam and Eve that they could no longer have contact with Him. Just as He had cast Lucifer away from Him when Lucifer disobeyed, God now had to do the same thing with Adam and Eve. He told them, in short, that their disobedience had spoiled everything, including the Garden itself. Man would now have to go outside the garden and work for everything he needed: food, shelter and clothing. No longer would God create men, but, starting with Eve, woman would have to bear the pain of childbirth. And so it is to this very day.

But God was sad. He created man to love and to share with Him, but they turned their backs on Him and His perfect laws.

They immediately saw what the results of eating from that tree were. But it was too late. Now God knew that they could not do anything to make amends for what they had done. So He took skins from the animals and covered them. This meant that an innocent animal had to die to cover them. Blood is life. God told man that the only way to have any contact with Him from then on was through blood. Man would have to sacrifice the life of something dear in order to reach God. Even though He was God, He could not go back on His own punishment and His own Word. But out of mercy and love, God found a way for man to stay in touch with Him.

Even so, the damage was done, and there was no turning back. When a child disobeys your rules, you punish him. You don't make up these rules out of the blue and for no reason. From age, wisdom and experience you have learned that some things can hurt your child. So you lay down rules and parameters to protect them. Just because nothing bad happened the first time they disobeyed you does not mean something worse might not happen the next time. So you punish them to teach them a lesson. They can never take back what they have done, but, out of love, you let them know that you still love them. But you do not change the rules to show them this.

It is the same with God, but to a much greater degree. From then on, sacrifice became an integral part of man's communication with God. I don't know about you, but if we still had to do that I would single-handedly put down an entire herd of cattle or something close to it every year!

So why, after some 4000 years, don't we have to do that anymore? After your child reaches a certain age, you cut back on the rules a little so they can start to practice what they have been taught. You can love them and raise them to the best of your ability, but the day will come when they will have to have free will to do either right or wrong. You have to let them go. You cannot keep them under your wing forever. And so it is with God. He knew man's very nature was sin because of what happened in the garden. We all sin and fall short of the Glory of God. No matter how hard we try we fail. The flesh is so very weak. God saw this and did something amazing.

CHAPTER 4
The Principals of Faith

How can I believe in someone I cannot even see? In the previous chapter I addressed how man (we) betrayed God by listening to lies and disobeying God's only law at the time. I told how we had broken our fellowship and direct contact with our Father, God, and that how as a result, the very earth itself was defiled. The garden was off limits, and man had to go out into the wilderness and make the soil produce food, clothing, and shelter.

So maybe now you are starting to see that our being betrayed, broken and defiled was not God's fault. Nor was it your fault. It is a result of a natural course of events that started at the beginning of the world itself. It is called sin. As a result of Satan meeting with man at the water cooler, the very thing that you have endured or are still enduring has happened or is still happening. But as you will see, what God did next shows that He still knows us and loves us all.

Now we come to the question of believing in a spirit that we cannot even see. This is called having faith. In the seventies, the expression "Keep the faith, baby" became very popular. The definition of faith is the *substance of things hoped for and the evidence of things not seen.* Stop and think for a moment, and be honest about it. Life itself is one big act of faith after another. We have faith that we will do everything from waking up in the morning to finding a job to living to a ripe old age. Believing in our spiritual Father is an act of faith as well.

I take you back to the Big Bang Theory. In a nutshell, this theory asks us to accept that primeval atoms broke apart into a billion particles and kept expanding and expanding into the universe we have today. As far as I am concerned, until one of those scientists can explain to me where that original mass of dense particles came from, I will continue to have faith in my heavenly Father. And contrary to the belief that we are just a mass of people reproducing at the speed of light down here with no purpose to our lives, and that we are all just accidents of nature, God knows each one of us. He has given each of us work to do on earth. Controlling and making the lives of other human beings miserable is not what it is, either.

Everything I am going to tell you now will take faith to listen to and to accept. Your free will comes into play here. This book was written to make you take a stand for your own life and destiny, and to help you choose how the rest of your life is going to be.

Now let us move forward some 4000 years. God knew that man, because of his knowledge of good and evil and because of the weakness of the flesh, would forever have to make blood sacrifices as they had been doing since Adam and Eve sold out. He also knew that blood sacrifices would be extremely difficult to continue. And He wanted to do something once and for all to reestablish His fellowship with man and to pay for all sins of all men, past, present, and future. He had to do this and still protect man's free will. He also could not sacrifice his own integrity which is perfect. So He decided to send His only Son to be the final sacrifice, the ultimate and final blood sacrifice that would free us all forever. And all we would have to do to be forgiven would be to accept this final blood sacrifice of Jesus Christ for the forgiveness of our sins. This solution would get around man's weak flesh and still give man free will to accept or reject the final sacrifice.

You must strap on your faith belt here. You must remember that God is just that, God. We too often try to make Him mere man to understand Him. We cannot do that. The basis of Christianity is that there is one God, and in that one God there are three, distinct and separate beings. There are three beings in one. Now this becomes less confusing for us if we just stop and think that God and His Son Jesus and the Holy Spirit are spirits. They are not flesh, although Christ became flesh for his mission on earth. They live in a real place but on a different level than the one we live on. Sounds like a combination of Star Trek and the Twilight Zone, doesn't it? But it is faith that will get us through this basic lesson of Christianity together.

So God is now ready to pay the ultimate price for our original sin that separated us from Him once and for all. He is going to pay the price Himself. Sometimes, here in our society, our kids may do something like destroy property. It is left up to the judge whether the child will be sent to jail, charged and released to your supervision, or perhaps, if you, the parent, pay for the damage, the child will not be charged and there will be no record of his offense. That is what God, our Father, decided to do for us. He would pay the price. He, in His perfect integrity went through the very channels He had established for Adam and Eve to produce another life. God could have zapped Jesus into being, but because He had originally sent man to earth to have rule and dominion over this earthly kingdom, it would have to be a human man that won it back from the thief Satan.

Prepare yourself: here is another speed bump for your faith. The third person of God, the Holy Spirit, provided the human chromosomes necessary to impregnate Mary. This had to be the Son of God, and yet God could not mingle in a physical manner with a human woman. So this miracle took place with Mary in order to produce the final sacrifice, Jesus Christ. There was never any physical contact. In fact, when the angel appeared to Mary and informed her that she was pregnant and that she was to call the child Jesus, she asked how this could be because she had never known a man. She was told that she had found favor with God. She had to strap on her seat belt of faith too! There were many wonders and miracles that took place from there on for Mary and Joseph, but we will leave those for another time. I want you to meet Jesus, the One who died for us.

Better tighten that seat belt another notch here. Some people will admit to the existence of Jesus on earth. There are actual historical accounts of His existence. But these only point to Jesus as an ordinary, flesh and blood person, no different than you and I. The miracle of the story of Jesus, and of His life and resurrection, is that He was God made flesh. Although it was God that sent His only Son to earth to accomplish remission of sin, Jesus was truly flesh and blood and knew of God only as His heavenly Father, as we do today. You see, it had to be a human being that paid with his life to regain the authority and ownership of this, our earthly Kingdom. Adam failed. If Christ had failed, well, I guess you and I would still be slicing up Fluffy and Spot to stay in contact with God. Some people say that it was no big deal for Jesus to die on the cross. That He was actually God and did not suffer at all. This is not true. Jesus was truly flesh. On the cross itself, Jesus lifted His eyes toward heaven and asked the question, "Father, why have you forsaken me?" I assure you that he felt every wound inflicted on Him and died for you and I of His own free will. Jesus, because of his communication with His heavenly Father, knew what His job here on earth was. Just as I told you, God has a job here on earth for each of us to do.

But when you become a Christian, you discover your purpose for your existence just as Jesus did. His was the hardest mission to be accepted from God. We all have things to do here for our Heavenly Father, but Jesus became aware of His purpose and that this purpose would require Him giving His life for you and me even though we had not even been born yet. I know of no one in my acquaintances that would be up to an assignment like that. Jesus knew that He had to call on the Holy Spirit to give Him strength and to enable Him to perform miracles through contact with His Father. He was not some magician that invited people to a matinee every day to perform tricks for their amusement. He was showing them the great love that their Heavenly Father had for them.

The people of that time had become, after 4000 years, trapped by religion. The Ten Commandments had become more than what was simply stated. The commandments became subject to man's interpretation and use. And religion became a weapon of man, used under the guise of God's will, to control others. Man had started interpreting God's word to suit himself, and Jesus was there to set His Father's laws straight. This made enemies. Just as it is in our world today, someone breaks the law and we hear them give their own interpretation of the law so that it suits their decision to do what they did and why they did it. Jesus said that if people would follow His example, then He would fulfill the law as they knew it. There were laws then for everything the Jews did. From the way that they dressed to cleanliness to food preparation and sacrifices to the way they prayed. Jesus was going to change all that.

But instead of following Christ's example, all the religious leaders could think of was the unemployment line waiting for them. Despite their threats, Jesus did persevere and showed others the way back to His Father. He persevered all the way to

His death on the cross. God allowed His Son to die, to be the final sacrifice, the ultimate sacrifice, and to pay the ultimate price for sin. From the cross, as people still mocked Him and cast lots for His clothes, He looked up toward heaven and asked His Father to "forgive them for they know not what they do."

That was the miracle. Both you and I know that if God was our Father we would be asking Him to let us down from that cross and give us the power to whoop their ungrateful butts! But Jesus in His perfect humility and obedience saw His trial through to the end. His last words were, "It is finished." And with that, He bought our freedom. Freedom for you and me and everyone who is willing to do just one very simple thing: accept what Jesus did for us. We have to accept Jesus as our Lord and Savior. Then, on the day when the final judgment of God is held, when our sins are presented, Jesus will step up and tell His Father that He has paid our debt. Just as the earthly court will find no blame in the child that committed no crime because the fine was paid by his father, God will find you and me blameless because the price was paid for by the Blood of our Savior, Jesus Christ. Christ hands us our "Get out of jail free" card.

The true miracle of Jesus' sacrifice is not that Jesus said some beautiful and brave words and allowed the soldiers to nail Him to the cross. He did what any human being would have done if nailed to a cross for six hours after a terrible beating and that was to die. The miracle was that He arose again. He returned to His Father. But He did one very important thing first. He went looking for Satan, who had stolen the keys to the kingdom of earth from Adam and Eve all those thousands of years before. Jesus took the keys back and informed Satan that although he would still be able to hang around earth, where he had been cast down, he *no longer* had the *authority* to rule and reign. Jesus, by His death and Resurrection, had bought that authority back. And then after He had done this he returned to His disciples to prove his resurrection. Mortal man cannot do this.

It just amazes me that more people will not come to the realization of their Savior. It has been said, "I would rather live my life as if there were a God and find out that there was none, than live my life as though there was no God and find out that there was." I do not know who said this, but it is so true. But just believing in God is not enough. You must accept His sacrifice in order to choose eternal life. You are going to have eternal life either way, but the alternative is too horrible to think of.

So today, even when he knows better, Satan still tempts human flesh to sin and fall short of what God expects and demands that we do. But the difference now is that we can finally really "kick some butt" and tell Satan that we prefer to follow the One that returned dominion over this earth to us. We do not have to put up with Satan and his tormenting little imps and demons that run to and fro seeking someone to destroy. Once you accept Christ, you have an advocate, an attorney, who will fight your battles for you. God is in communication with you again through the sacrificial Blood of His Son. Your attorney fees have been paid in advance and in full. He will send you supernatural help in your time of need and be the best Father anyone could hope to have. If a mortal man can be a father and love his child, then how much more can God himself be as a Father? He can and is the perfect Father. This is why Christians are so excited. They have seen the miracles that are performed to this very day. They are recipients of those miracles. I don't care what obstacles come up in our lives, we can call on and get results from our Father. We do not have to go through any church official or perform any religious rite; we can go freely before the Father, through Jesus His Son, and make our confessions and requests known. And we see results. Not always the results that our carnal minds have come up with, but the results given to us from God. And I know first hand that some solutions come from what we refer to as "out of the blue." That is why they are miraculous to me.

Now this understanding that I have given you is so simple. But you have, I am sure, many questions about God and Jesus. Once you come to the Lord, there is so much that will be at your disposal to help you learn more about Jesus and His life here on earth. You will also see that Jesus, as God made flesh, was *betrayed* by Judas and the murmurings of the religious factions of His day, *broken* by the fists and whips of the Roman interrogators, and *defiled* by those who taunted Him and cast lots for his clothing as He hung dying on the cross.

To sum God and Jesus up in one word, it is *love*. Their Word is love. We will still sin. We will still fall. But Jesus will be there to pick us up. He will dust us off and will set our feet straight on the correct path once again. And we accept this all by faith. That is how you believe and trust in someone that you cannot see. And if you are honest with yourself, you will have to admit that it takes a lot more faith to trust the word of another human being. Will there still be trials in life? You bet. But the difference now is that you are no longer alone and subject to what Satan hands out. He is here illegally. I heard Myles Munroe, an amazing preacher and teacher; refer to Satan as nothing more than an unemployed cherub. And even though a man may break the law, the one who led him to break the law (Satan) is responsible, too. You will have to pay your earthly fine, but heaven will no longer remember this transgression. However, the end of Satan's story is eternal damnation. On the other hand, when you confess your sin it is removed as far as the East is from the West. God no longer remembers your confessed sin. It would be great if we could forget the bad things that we have done. This is where the devil enters in again by trying to tell us that we are bad and not forgiven. But God's word says that He no longer remembers our confessed sins. And remember, His word is perfect.

Where you may have walked with Satan before, you are now free by the Blood of Jesus. What a comfort that is. Now, this does not mean that we can stop trying to fight temptation. Because we are flesh, we will still have to face this battle every day for the rest of our lives, and God expects us to do so earnestly. It is like when, certain times of the year, charities and churches make needs like food and gifts, etc., free for the asking. They trust that only the needy will show up. However, there are some that feel they can come and take the free things, even though they can well afford them. But we cannot take a free ride on the Blood of Jesus. We must know what is right and wrong and try to stay on the right path. If you love someone, anyone, you always try to impress them and to please them. How much more should we do for the one that gave His life for us and for our Heavenly Father who gave Him to us?

CHAPTER 5
Action Enables the Invisible to Work in the Visible

How can someone invisible get me out of the mess I am in?

After His death, Jesus reappeared to His disciples and to others to confirm His resurrection. Even those who were closest to Him had trouble believing that He could rise again. Even Thomas, one of His disciples thought that the other disciples were pulling his leg when they told him that Jesus had risen. Jesus appeared to Thomas personally and had him put his fingers into His wounds to prove to him that He was alive again. This is where the expression "Doubting Thomas" comes from. So even after we, as Christians, accept Jesus and what He has done for us, it is still hard to believe that someone whom we cannot see is able to do things on our behalf. You might as well know that all of us, each and every day, rely on our faith in God as much as we rely on Him to help us. I assure you, you will see the results of your faith. Therefore, having faith and belief becomes as easy as getting dressed every day.

The first thing you must train your brain to say and believe is that you cannot do or say anything to strengthen yourself without Jesus. Can you go over and pick up that book on the table? Yes. But can you just put down a pack of cigarettes and never touch them again? Can you never touch a drop of booze ever again if you are an alcoholic? Can you get off the streets if you are owned and controlled by a pimp that will beat or kill you for leaving? Can you get off of drugs cold turkey? *No, you can't.* Not only can you not do it, but you cannot even get to the point that you will consider it possible! So, your first step is to say, "I can do all things *through* Christ who strengthens me." I told you before that if you think that you can defeat anything in the devil's territory by yourself and in the flesh you are sadly mistaken, and you will be in grave peril. So never attempt to do anything by yourself. If you start out to do any of the above and you call on Christ first, He will make the impossible possible. You, by those words, will enable the Invisible to work in the Visible.

You can ask God to deliver you from your current circumstances, but you must take some steps yourself. God gave you a mind, a body, and a soul, so now is the time to use them. *First*, you have to accept the sacrifice that Jesus made for you. You must accept Him as your personal Lord and Savior (instructions to do this are at the end of the book). *Second*, you must expose Satan by telling him to get behind you—you are now a child of the living God. Bulletin! God is not dead, and Christ has risen again and sits at the right hand of His Father. Let Satan, who despite popular belief is not a monster in a movie, nor is he dead, he was never alive to begin with, but is at the top of the evil spirit list; know that you now are a child of the living God. He has been duping mankind for thousands of years into the belief that either there is no God at all, or that God is dead or that Jesus died but did not rise again. Lies from the pits of hell! Inform Satan that you are no longer in the market for the lies that have kept you apart from God.

Third, you must realize that God has had His hand on you all along or else you would be dead, either because of your own destructive behavior or by the hands of those with whom you associate. You must remove yourself from your current environment. Jesus helped people who wanted to leave their bad circumstances but were unable to accomplish it on their own. One day in Jerusalem, He came to the Pool of Bethesda, where many of the city's lame and blind and crippled would camp. Miracles happened in this pool. On occasion, the water would be stirred by the hand of an angel, and whoever got into the water first was healed. Jesus approached a man who lay a distance from the water. This man had been crippled for thirty-eight years. Jesus did not ask him for any reasons that he may have had for not being healed; He simply asked the man if he *wanted* to be healed. The man replied that in order to be healed, he would have to get into the water. But as it was never known when the pool would be stirred, by the time he would summon help, someone else had always made it into the water before him. Sternly, Jesus told him to pick up his mat and walk! The man was healed at once. You must ask Jesus to help you change your circumstances. You must truly want it more than anything else. You must move when doors open for you, but you must be looking for the doors in the first place.

God knows where you have been. Just as Jesus knew the circumstances of the man by the pool, God knows your circumstances. He just wants to save you and bring you out of your mess. You need to take action and take it immediately. Take up *your* mat and be healed! Your action enables God to work in your life. Your environment is contagious. If it stinks, get out. You need, if you are on the streets, to get yourself to the nearest mission. They can direct you to safe houses and help you make your transitions. If you are in any other situation that allows you to get you to a church, by all means, run, do not walk, to them and ask them for help. They will direct you to many sources that can help you. Once you have done this, don't look back. Make up your mind that you will never go backward ever again. If you only go one foot forward, at least you have not gone back and that is progress and that is something that you can be proud of.

Keep in mind that Satan will fight you all the way here. Whether you are trying to get away from a pimp, drugs or an emotional and or physically abusive relationship, Satan knows what strings to pull. He knows how to make you feel guilty. He will tell you the biggest lie, even through family and close friends, that you cannot change or be anything. You are just a loser and failure. Lies from the pits of hell again!

God will work supernaturally to help you accomplish this. He will send people into your life to help you. He will enable you to stop allowing people to run your life. He will enable you to stop your self-destructive lifestyle. He will enable you to love yourself and respect yourself again, and lastly He will enable you to let go and let God. Christ won on the cross. You are now a winner. You are not, nor were you ever, responsible for what happened to you. You don't have to listen to any negative talk about you or your trials. Through trials come wisdom. You now know the things that the enemy will send you. God will teach you and supernaturally help you to avoid all the arrows of the enemy, whether that is Satan or your tormentor(s) who are controlled by Satan. So make plans and implement them now.

This is where you lock up with doubt and fear, isn't it? Jesus once told His disciples that they could do anything and have authority over everything in their lives if they only had faith. In fact, He told them that if they had faith as small as a mustard seed they could say to a mountain, "Be moved," and the mountain would move. Faith, faith, faith. I cannot stress this enough.

I am not just talking to those of you outside of the will of

God. I am also talking here to so many that sit in pews today that have given your life to Jesus. You know Him. You know the miracles He performs. You have seen His power first hand and yet you sit there full of hate and sorrow and, because of this, your work for the Lord is limited. You are not reading this book by some fluke. God has put this book in front of you to bring you back to Him or to make you stronger and heal you as a Christian. When I stated earlier that every person in every pew has a story, some of the stories are about abuse. And this will be a surprise to the world, but not everyone sitting in a pew in church on Sunday is truly saved because they are the abusers and continue to abuse on a regular basis. When you accept Christ as your Lord and Savior, you are to become a new person. And you have the strength of God himself to help you become this new, whole, and healed person. He knows how badly you hurt and how you were *betrayed*, by another human being, and how your spirit was *broken*, and how your body has been *defiled*, by your tormentor(s). And although it is probably the hardest thing for you to do, you must consider the fact that your abuser was probably abused and needs help to come out of his or her abusing as much as you the abused need healing from your experiences. To tell you that it is over is not a hope or a wish for you, but a fact. I am writing this to tell you that He created you and loves you and that He is the Father you can love and trust. You can climb up in His lap and not fear for anything. He will always be with you. *HE WILL NEVER LEAVE YOU OR FORSAKE YOU.* Your wisdom that you have gained through your great trials will be turned to your benefit. God will see to it, that what the enemy intended as evil will be turned for good.

It would truly grieve God to see you continue to struggle through life in your current circumstances. He is offering you a new life. He will see to the punishment and destruction of your enemies if they do not turn from their evil ways. Everyone in this country has access to radio, television, books, and churches. Whether they will admit it or not, they have heard someone offer them the chance to give their life to the Lord. God knows those who will come to Him and those who will not. So you need to turn these offenders over to God, and He will handle them. And yes, God can handle them through the legal system. I am telling you right here and now that the solution is yours for the taking. It is so simple and it is free. You don't have to clean up your life first. If you wait until that happens, you will never ever come to Christ. You are flesh and blood, and you can never ever get "right" enough to please God. That is why that price was already paid.

If you have not already done so, turn to the back of this book now and say the Sinner's Prayer. Give your life to Jesus now and just watch your life change. I am not saying that you will not still have issues in your life. But from the day you say that prayer, and mean it, you will never fight another battle alone again. And when your life is through and you, as we all will, stand before God on Judgment Day, and God asks you about your sins and transgressions, Jesus will step forward, put his loving arm around your shoulder and say "Father, this is one of mine, whose debt has been paid by the shedding of my blood." God will say no more but welcome you into eternal life with Him. Do not pay with your own soul for what others did to you! REMEMBER THIS. DO NOT PAY FOR WHAT OTHERS DID TO YOU WITH YOUR OWN SOUL! Stop the roller coaster now and get off, before it is too late.

Someone I once was close to was abused as a child by their father. I am intentionally not mentioning gender here. This person has deluded themselves into thinking that what happened to them was not that bad and that it really does not bother them. But if this is the case, then why is this person a functioning alcoholic? Why have they drunk so much over the years that the doctors have told them that if they drink any more they will die? This person says that no penetration ever happened but that the father would just lie on the bed and rub his erection on them. THIS IS ABUSE!! And to be in such denial is not healthy. You are not bothered? Then why does your spouse feel that you are so cold and so distant? Why have you been drinking yourself to death? YOU NEED HELP. This person is so ill that they actually seem to be envious of the other child in that family that was molested by penetration. They seem to think that their sibling got more attention than they did. This person believes in Christ, as do their family and children. They have mocked the "born again" Christians over and over. I think this person needs to re-acquaint themselves with God, go to church, and seek help.

You can be saved and be assured that heaven is yours. Why give the devil your good life when he does not even have any legal right to it? What has he done to deserve such a gift from you? You see, just as you are free to give your life to Christ or reject the offer, you are just as free to hand your life over to Satan. Why would you do this when such freedom awaits you through Jesus Christ? Satan never died for you. He has never done one thing for you except to seek you out to steal, kill and destroy you. That is all Satan is capable of. Your life is very short but very precious too. It is time for you to find God. And it is time to live for Him and know that He still performs miracles today.

CHAPTER 6
How and Why Must I Forgive

How do I forgive the people that have hurt me, and why do You ask this of me?

Forgiving those who have hurt us physically, emotionally, and spiritually is perhaps the most difficult thing we will have to do as Christians. Although our souls and spirits have shifted gears, this flesh still knows what hate is. Like I told you before, hate only works on the hater. It will eat away at your mind, body, and soul like slow-moving lava if you let it. It may take a long time to destroy you, but destroy you it will. You will have to rely on the "new man" that you have become through Christ. You should take great, great pride in this fact. You are brand new in Christ. You are changing your environment, perhaps your address, and your friends and old acquaintances that are a part of your life prior to your becoming "Born Again". You don't have to give up all your friends, but you will naturally want to get away from those that are destructive to your life. Not only are they destructive now, but, if you will be truly honest, they were a very destructive influence all along. However, you will find yourself telling your friends all about your new experience with God. Some will mock, and laugh and try and intimidate you back into your old lifestyle. But remember this, for all the things that these people say they can do for you they cannot save your soul. And your soul is your eternity. Make no mistake. There are no parties in hell.

And to quote a gentleman by the name of Paul Crouch, "Just what in hell do you want anyway?"

I mentioned before that *all* have fallen short and have sinned. And just because you become a Christian does not mean that you will no longer sin. Your temptations will even be stronger. I'm sure we have all asked ourselves why some of the most terrible people in the world seem to have it all and never seem to have any problems. Satan does not come against those he already claims as his. Why should he? They are living greedy, lustful, hateful lives away from God. It is when you have been part of Satan's world and go over to the other (winning) side that the devil gets angry. He will try to get you back at all costs. And he will throw everything in his bag at you.

But remember, you can do all things through Christ who strengthens you. Jesus will throw love and help and strength and angels into your life to help you. Christ died so that we would have life and have it more abundantly. He does not want us to be miserable. And please believe me, I know what it is to hate, and it made me miserable. Those you hate don't care that you hate them. Their souls are so ugly that they actually feed on your anger and hatred. When you hate them, you are still playing their game even if you have removed yourself from them. You need to turn these people over to God and ask God to help you forgive them. In God's eyes, your sins are just as terrible as those of your abusers. To God, sin—any sin—is all the same. There is no degree that makes one sin greater than the other. All who sin will be punished, either here or most certainly in the afterlife. It doesn't seem fair, does it? But you are thinking with the mind of man. When the end comes, hell will be waiting for all sinners.

I had to pray for divine intervention when it came to

releasing my hatred. I forgave my father after I became a Christian and tried to do all that a good daughter should do. It was the hardest thing I ever did. But it helped me go on with my parents. After the death of my father, I realized that the hate was still well and alive in me. And I cried after he died. Not because he was dead, but because he had cheated me out of my father. He had cheated me out of a normal life. And I realized toward the end of his life that his love for me was that of a man for a woman and not as a father for a child.

I let this fester for years after my father died in 1995. I finally understood that this bitterness and hatred was keeping me from a full relationship with Christ. I truly wanted that as much as I wanted and needed peace and closure. It wasn't until the Holy Spirit gave His urging for me to write this book that I knew that I had to write it free of hatred if I were to reach you. You are so very important to God and to me, His servant forever. In prayer I asked God to help me to truly forgive my father so that I could go on with my life to its fullest.

Suddenly, God let me see myself with my dad before the molesting started. This is what I mean about having access to God once you accept Jesus as your Lord and Savior. I saw my dad clearly. He had his head back and was laughing. He was the beautiful hero that I once knew. And I felt again the enormous love that I once had for him. Tears came to my eyes and I said out loud, "I love you, Daddy. What happened to you? Where did you go?" I realized that my loathing was now directed at Satan, who had stolen my father's very soul.

In that moment of intense love, forgiveness was enabled by God. In that moment I forgave my father and was set free. Free to love myself for the first time in years. Free to get more help. Free to love others, and my husband, to the degree that they deserved to be loved. To appreciate life, love and God to the maximum that man can know love.

This is why it is so important to forgive. So please don't wait all the years I waited to find the true ability to forgive. One of the first requests you should make of God is for the ability to forgive. If you are still aware of or are in contact with your abuser(s), you can smile at them with an understanding that can only come from God and tell them that you forgive them. It will set you free. Make sure that you tell them that you are turning them over to God, and then go about your new life to its fullest. Whom God sets free is free indeed! God says that if we want our enemies blessed, then we should curse them. If we want them cursed, then we should pray for them. In other words, vengeance is the Lord's. We are not made to handle hate. God has such wonderful things in store for you; hate is not one of them. Let Him take care of your enemies. Remember the things that God did in his righteous anger to those who harmed his own or came against him. Remember the story of Moses? I want someone who parted the Red Sea to handle my enemies. He can do a much better job than I can or you can. So let's just concentrate on love from now on.

CHAPTER 7
Your New Identity

Once I put these terrible things behind me, will I ever have peace and be able to live a good life? What is the revelation that will stop this living hell?

Hold your head up. I don't care where you have come from and neither does God. You are now a son or daughter of the living God. You have a scar, but now Christ has changed that scar into a testimony. When Christ died on the cross for you, His body was *broken*. When He reappeared to His disciples in His new and glorified body, it still had the scars of His horrible ordeal. But now He showed His scars as His testimony. He was Christ, the Son of the Living God. He, willingly and of His free will, was *betrayed, broken, and defiled* so that we may have life everlasting with Him and His Father. His resurrection enabled us to now and forever be free from the price of death for our sins. We are now and forever brothers and sisters of Jesus Christ Himself. We, too, once we have accepted Jesus as our Lord and Savior, become new people. Our past lives are the scars we bear, but those scars are now our testimony to the world. Will we look different? No. Will we sound different? No. But the joy of receiving all that Jesus' death supplies will shine through on our faces and in our everyday lives.

People were amazed at the change in me. Some asked if I did something to my hair. One person who had not seen me for a while actually asked if I had had a face-lift! Hate and anger and sorrow and worry and stress take their toll on our lives. A smile is amazing. And you will find yourself smiling a lot because you have a secret that you won't want to keep to yourself. Remember how those pesky Christians will just come up to you and start talking about redemption? Once you have it, you, too, will want to share it. You will want to go to the others you left behind and encourage them to find Christ.

Don't get me wrong; you will still have trials in your life. Sickness and strife are very much a part of the world that exists now because of Adam and Eve's bad decision. But once you have Christ, you have an advocate to the Father. You will see God do things in your life that will amaze you. You will be searching for a solution to a problem. And God will show you a solution that you would not have thought of in a thousand years.

Have you ever gone to the store and bought a barbeque grill, for instance? You open the box and there are a ton of nuts and bolts and pieces of metal. Now, there are a million possibilities for attaching parts to parts. But if you were to do it your way, there is no telling what you could come up with. However, if you take out the manual, it will very clearly and concisely tell you how to assemble the parts so you end up with what was intended by the manufacturer as a barbeque grill.

It is the same with life. People have mocked the Bible for centuries. Yet the Bible is God's manual for life itself! You have all the tools, but the Bible will tell you how to assemble your life so that it runs smoothly and so that it will get you back home to Him in the end. Since becoming a Christian, I have wondered how I made it before having His manual. Well, the answer is that I did a very poor job. In the end, it doesn't matter what was done to you in your life by others; it comes down to what you have done for yourself. You are the one that has responsibility for your life. For the sins you commit. You need to join me and reach out to others like us and bring them into a safe harbor. Let them know that the price was paid over 2000 years ago on Calvary by our big brother, Christ Himself! Again I repeat myself by saying that if you do not do something about your life, and you continue without the free gift of God, you are bound to spend ETERNITY with your abuser and the one who has perfected hate and that is Satan himself.

Once we have given our lives to Christ, God has an assignment for us. God is the owner, so to speak, of earth. He is the King. This is why the Bible refers to earth as the Kingdom. Jesus told everyone about the Kingdom of God while He was here on earth. To this day, even some Christians believe that when the Bible refers to the Kingdom of God that the Bible is speaking of heaven. Remember that the earth is an extension of heaven. God created a "kingdom" here on earth. When Jesus taught His disciples to pray properly he told them to say, "Our Father, who art in heaven, hallowed be thy name." We are to give God praise and worship for who He is. "Thy kingdom come, and Thy will be done, on earth as it is in heaven." We are affirming His kingdom here on earth. "Give us this day our daily bread." Here we acknowledge that God provides everything we need to sustain ourselves in our earthly lives. "And forgive us our trespasses, as we forgive those who trespass against us." Here is forgiveness again. Remember, God says that if we are to be forgiven, we must forgive others. And this is vital to having our prayers answered. You must come to the Father with a true and pure heart that is void of malice. "And lead us not into temptation." God is not going to lead us into temptation. But sin, too, is a part of life now, thanks to Adam and Eve. (I have had a lot of people tell me that Adam and Eve are the first people that they want to look up once they get to heaven. They want to kick their butts! I, too, have thought of this!) So with this line of the Lord's Prayer, we are asking for the strength to avoid sin in our daily lives. "But deliver us from evil." This is asking God to protect us from the wiles of Satan and his demons. Remember that they roam about seeking who they can steal from, kill and destroy. "For Thine, (God's) is the kingdom, the power, and the glory, forever and ever, Amen." This gives God praise and honor as the owner and King of the earth. We are acknowledging His power to help us while we are assigned here. We state that we will always give Him the glory for things He has done.

Notice that I say "assigned here." From the time we are born the devil sets about diverting our attention from God. Our first mission here on earth is to find our way back to our creator God. We now have to realize that when this has been accomplished, we have work to do for the Kingdom of Heaven. We are here as "Ambassadors" for the Kingdom of Heaven. God's children are lost and must be brought home. God has set down a very specific way for His children to come home, and this is the only way for them to do so. Remember, I told you that God's Word is so true and powerful that God, in his perfect integrity, must abide by it too. It is our responsibility as not only sons and daughters, but also as His ambassadors to see to the fulfillment of His wishes here on earth and to be representatives of heaven on earth. This includes introducing His most precious Son Jesus Christ to all the people in God's realm.

All countries have ambassadors. Did you know that when someone becomes an ambassador of a country that the life of that person becomes the responsibility of that country? All the debts of that person are paid for by that country. Even the allowances of the ambassador's children are paid for by the country that the ambassador represents. Again I remind you that if a country here on earth is that good at seeing to the life of its ambassador, how much more is God faithful to see to the needs of His ambassadors?

Are you starting to see how important you are in your Father's eyes? It gets better! One of the most beautiful paintings I have ever seen is one of Jesus, who is a shepherd, attending His many sheep. He leaves them all to find the one who has wandered off, the one that is lost, and the one that has not heard Him calling its name. When I was first saved, just looking at this painting made me cry. It made me feel so special. Because, as you well know, pure, unconditional love is what those of us who have been betrayed, broken and defiled need and want and crave the most. And I found this in Jesus Christ.

You can posture and pose and put on an act before humans; odds are you will be ignored for your efforts, or you will attract the very people that put you where you are because you are a product of your environment. You will never find true love until you find your God. He will teach you and allow you to find the "you" He sees. You will love the new you and you will then know how to truly love and be loved. You will feel special, and you deserve to feel special. Every one of us that has been called by God and accepts the call is eternally special. Because of this you will rejoice in the One who set you free!

If you look at the world we live in from God's perspective, it is very simple to figure out. You are either lost or found. The earth, God's creation, is not a mistake or a freak of nature. By the same argument, neither are you. You are in the place you are now because of natural events that must occur due to Adam and Eve's fall. It is *your* responsibility to look for your Father, and to respond when you hear His voice. He is out there, and He has called you by name. If you have not heard Him, then you were not listening.

PATTI THEISEN

I want you to know that you are being called by Him. His children know His voice. But remember free will. You can open the door for Him, or you can walk away. Tell me truthfully. If you got a summons from an earthly king, and he told you that if your accepted him as your king, he would give you everything that was his, what would you do? I'd take it! The truth that Satan does not want you to know is that the earth, right here where you live, is God's palace and not his. Satan stomped around in it for a while, but the moment Christ arose from the dead; he officially removed his authority over it. Although Satan is still slinking around, he has no authority. Once you accept God's call, you have the authority, through Christ, to tell Satan to get away from you, and to get his hands off God's people.

Ever have someone at work running around telling everyone what to do? You wonder if they really think that they are the boss. Mostly we just consider them fools. Well, the devil is a fool. Christ told him he was finished, but he still thinks that he can win. And the pity is that every time someone rejects Christ's gift of salvation, it puts another notch in Satan's belt.

Have you ever heard someone say, "I'm not worrying about going to hell because we're already in hell on earth"? Many believe that. But taking the hell out of your life is simple. Just by accepting Jesus and what He did on the cross for you, you inherit the Kingdom of Earth and Heaven, even though you were not made for heaven. You were made for earth. God, who is a spirit, never intended to come to earth. He put you and me here to run things and be His ambassadors to heaven. Now, if someone was trying to tear down your house or trash your yard, or steal your things, you would have a fit and do something about it. Well, our Father's kingdom is being ravaged daily, and it is up to us to change things. This is our property, and we are in charge of it. We will be richly rewarded by the King for how we represent Him and protect His property. His property includes you. You will be judged on how you care for yourself as well.

So take special pride in who you are in God's eyes. It does not matter what mortal man thinks of you. You have been handpicked by God Himself to represent Him. It is mind boggling when you think about it enormity of it all. We may have missed out on the love and respect that man could and should have given us, but when you think of what we have *survived,* we are the biggest winners of them all. We no longer have to be plagued by bad memories and hatred. We can now turn the offenders over to God and go on with our lives living for the God that created us and who will love us for all time. In God's perfection, He can love each one of us best. We may die one day in this flesh body, but our souls will soar with the eagles for eternity and we shall see the face of God. And yes, God will see to the destruction of those who hurt you.

The final and true realization of this Kingdom here on earth and our rightful place in it is what excites Christians, the adopted sons and daughters of the living God. We don't want to see others perish. We are not some supreme race, but humans just like you. We have suffered just like you. We bear the same scars just like you. But the One who came for us bears the greatest scars of all. By those scars we are saved, and by His stripes that He took on His back we are healed.

Yes, God is still in the miracle business. I have seen them. I have received many, both physical and emotional. And it was all free for the asking. Free because now when our Heavenly Father looks at me, He doesn't see me but the blood of His precious Son over me, blood that was shed for me and that I willingly accepted. Please stop suffering. Now is the time to accept this free gift. There are no strings attached. You have nothing to gain by walking away. Are you really that happy where you are? If you say yes, then I know as one of you that you are a liar. Does it seem that I am pushing here? Yes, I am pushing, because this is the only answer. Get good and mad for the last time over what has happened to you; get up from where you are right now, dust off the stench of what happened to you, and sign up as an ambassador of the Kingdom of God on earth! Look up, and in your mind's eye see the outstretched arms of your Savior. He is waiting for you. And when you run into His loving arms, the very angels of heaven will rejoice and write your name in the Lamb's Book of Life. Hell will writhe in agony at the loss of your soul. Did you ever think that the day would come that you would be so important to God? Did you ever think that the day would come when something you would do would shake the very foundations of hell itself? If you accepted Christ, it is exactly what you have done. You are a new creation in Christ!

CHAPTER 8
Prayers, Are They Answered?

Why have I gone through all of this? The last question I asked God was, "Why did you allow this to happen to me? Do you know what He said? His answer was, "Because you were strong enough." I could not believe that this was His answer! That seemed so cold to me. In fact, I got a little angry with God just then. I really don't know what I was looking for. Did I really think that God was going to apologize to me? My father refused to, so was God supposed to? Crazy, huh?

And now I imagine that you think one of my wheels has slipped off the track because I hear God's voice. But many hear His voice. Some have heard Him audibly, and others hear His direction in their mind and spirit. Yes, the spirit has ears. How do you get to hear from God? You pray. And there is a specific way you must pray in order to have your prayers listened to. I illustrated this by breaking down the Lord's Prayer in the previous chapter.

What does a best friend do for you? He or she will praise you. Tell you how great you are no matter what is going on in your life. He or she will build you up. And if they are a very good friend, they will do this often. We all need friendship in our lives to make our lives full. God is the same way. He wants to hear from you. He wants your praise. He wants your time and fellowship. He created man to be an extension of Him.

Remember that He enjoyed coming in the spirit to visit Adam and Eve in the Garden of Eden. And the day when they sinned and hid from Him made Him very sad. Some Christians—I call them part-time Christians—ignore God unless something goes wrong or they need something. How would you feel about someone that only showed up and said nice things to you because they wanted something? I know you have had this happen to you. We have all experienced this, and it makes us feel used. It takes enormous gall to do this to our Heavenly Father, and yet to some degree, we are all guilty of this.

I have made it not a practice but a joy to begin and end my days with prayer, worship, and fellowship with my Father in heaven. It sets my feet on the right path every day. "Good morning, Father, good morning, Jesus, good morning, Holy Spirit," is how I start each new day. My husband and I also put on what is called *the full armor of God* before we go out into the world. It is our spiritual protection against the old booger that still thinks he is in charge. We don't leave home without it. A copy of the prayer we say is in the back of this book. My husband took it from Ephesians chapter six in the Bible. It works. Once you accept Jesus (remember that we have no communication with the Father except through his son Jesus) and start a regular and consistent prayer life, you, too, will hear from God.

But be prepared. Because God sees and knows everything, He knows what is best for you and sometimes His answer will be no. But He will show you another way. You must trust in Him with all your heart, soul and mind. He will never leave you or forsake you. Some people don't give a second thought to prayer. But think about it. You are in contact with *God Himself* and not some Genie whose lamp you are rubbing to gain three wishes.

So make it a practice to start your day with God. It should become as natural to you as eating breakfast. First be still. Be quiet and know that it is God that you are going to speak to. Start by giving Him all the adoration that is in your heart, for He is the author of your very existence. Tell God of your shortcomings and sins. Let Him know that they bother you and that you are sorry for offending Him by giving in to the flesh. Never forget that you are human and that you are going to make mistakes. We all make mistakes. We try very hard not to, but sin we do! Give God thanks for His forgiveness. How do you know He has forgiven you? We have His Word for that, too. Remember His perfect INTEGRITY? God will never break a promise He has made. He said that if we would confess our sins to Him, He would be faithful to forgive us and put us in "right standing" with Him again. What a promise.

Now, this does not mean that we can go out and do whatever we feel like and say to ourselves, "God must forgive me." God is not a fool, and you would be a fool to try and make one out of Him. He knows your heart and your motives. He requires true repentance and a true effort not to sin again in order to forgive you.

As I stated before, as you start to hear from God, you will know that things you are doing are wrong. They could be things that you have been doing and thought nothing of at all, but now that you are hearing from God you see that what you have been doing is displeasing to Him. You must agree with Him and turn yourself around. Now that you have been forgiven, you must give thanks for His forgiveness. Thank Him for the blood sacrifice of His only Son Jesus that allows you to ask for forgiveness and be granted forgiveness. You no longer have to offer animals to worship God because the blood sacrifice of Jesus did that for you already. You just need to worship Him with praise and thanksgiving.

Have you ever been in debt to someone? Have you ever
been in the position that you could not pay the person back
on time? And have you ever had someone either give you more
time or tell you to just forget it all together? What a relief it
would be to either have more time or to learn that you did
not have to pay the debt back at all. You would smile and
probably say, "Thank you so very much; you don't know what
this means to me." It is the same feeling after you confess to
God. So let go with a big thank you to your Heavenly Father
for forgiving you.

Now you can make requests of God. He knows you have
concerns and needs, but you must ask for His help. You see, God
set the earth up so that He cannot do anything here unless we
ask Him to get involved. When He told us to have dominion
over the earth, He meant just that. There goes His perfect
integrity again. He actually says that whenever two or more
Christians are gathered in His name, and agree on something
on earth, it will be done in heaven. God will take action. This
doesn't mean that someone you don't like will instantaneously
go up in flames. But it does mean that if you are listening to
God and asking for things that are not contrary to His nature,
He will see to their fulfillment in your life.

We just don't realize how good we have it, nor do we
realize the power we have through Christ! God will answer your
prayers and requests in His own time. So if you ask something
of God and hit a stopwatch, you may be there for a while. And
yet, it could be answered almost immediately. God's timing
may not be our timing, but God *always* arrives *just* in time!

God also loves it when we remind Him of His promises
to us. That is why it is important that you get and read a
Bible. Be specific with God in your requests. Again, remember
that you have a free will, and God is only faithful to answer

requests that you have actually made to Him. So don't take a shortcut and say, "Hi, God, You know everything about me and You know what I want and need, so I will cut this short and You get busy." It won't work. When you go before God in prayer, you go as a proud child of a King. You go as a Prince or Princess before your Father the King. You are His creation, so don't start your prayer with, "Oh, God, here I am this lowly little worm in your presence." You are His child, His creation and don't ever forget what you are in His eyes! You cannot expect to have your prayers answered if you go to Him full of bitterness and hatred. Remember, you must forgive in order to be forgiven. If you are having a hard time forgiving someone, then ask others to pray for you and with you to overcome this stumbling block between you and your Father.

Sometimes we are so weary and tired when we go to God in prayer, overpowered by the things of this world, that we are at a total loss as to what to say or how to pray. When Jesus left the earth, He told his disciples that "another" would come in His place until He returned. He would be the "Comforter." This is the third person of God: the Holy Spirit. He is the gentle, loving sweetness of God. All you have to do is call on Him and tell Him that you need help, and He will fill your spirit with the right things to say to God.

A few years after I was saved, I read a book written by Benny Hinn called *Good Morning Holy Spirit*. I would like to suggest that you read this book to fully understand the nature of the precious Holy Spirit. Knowledge of Him will be a constant reminder, to strive to keep sin out of your life. Your behavior can very easily offend Him. Once you are aware of His loving presence, you will instantly notice when He leaves. Always feel free to call on Him, for He, too, will always answer.

I always end my prayers with the sentence, "In Jesus' name

I ask, Amen." When Jesus was here on earth, He said that whatever we would ask of the Father in His name, it would be done unto us. Again, don't ask for anything that would be outside the desires of God or anything that would offend Him. But I think you know that by now. Never forget what Jesus did for you. Never attempt to contact the Father without going through Jesus and using His name. And what a privilege that in itself is. Remember that you are special and that you have the right and privilege to be in contact with God through Christ. Many people who have not accepted Jesus cry out for God when they are in peril, and their requests fall on deaf ears. Frightening isn't it? Use what I have told you about to start and strengthen your prayer life. Do it every day and rejoice always in your right in Christ to do so. Talk to your Father every day, and you will hear from Him.

"You were strong enough," was what I heard from God. I asked God what He meant by His response. I heard the words, "The sins of the father." I knew then what it meant. I was under the same laws that all men are under. That is why bad things happen to good people and even children, remember? I survived because God saw in me someone that was strong and someone who would fight and not become like my molester. "The sins of the father" refers to the very things that you and I have gone through. Remember that sometimes people become just like their molesters? The sins of the father are passed down from generation to generation. It can be broken. Someone has to stand up and say, *enough is enough! This is not going to happen anymore. Not while I have something to say about it.* God knows that you were strong enough to survive too. You can now rely on God to take what the devil meant for evil and turn it for the good through you.

This is where you and I come in. We make it stop. We

defeat Satan here and now. Just as God is the author of our lives, Satan is the author of all we endure here on earth. If you say there is no devil, then you will be an easy target. Bad things just don't happen out of the blue. And they are not caused by God. Yes, God has perfect wrath, but He does not use it against His own children. God is not capable of encouraging murder, rape, theft, anger, rage and strife. These fall squarely on the shoulders of the devil. He first displayed this character in heaven when he turned on God. Do not ever forget how treacherous he is and that he will do anything and everything to derail you and your work for God. But "greater is He that is in you than he that is in the world." In other words, God is far greater than Satan, even though you could not convince Satan of that fact. God will direct our steps once we come out of the world and into His. He knew from the foundations of time that *you* would come home. And with this knowledge, He has made plans for you once you are His again.

I have such empathy with those like myself. I know that the devil wants to keep you exactly where you are. In the end, he wants to claim your soul and keep it in torment for eternity. I know that I have a passion for lost souls. I want to reach you all. Please consider carefully all the things that I have written in this book. Your life depends on it. Please rely on the resources in the back of this book to get yourself saved and started in a new direction. I love you even though I don't know you, and I know that our Heavenly Father loves you, too. He has spoken, I have written, and now the rest is up to you. Please make the right decision. Once you have, I know that you will be as excited as I am in knowing that we can do something together to rid the earth of this plague one offender at a time. I will be praying for you all.

CHAPTER 9
You Will Never Walk Alone

If you have made it this far through the book I am so excited for you. You have already made or are about to make the single most important decision in your life: to turn your life over to your Father in heaven by giving your life to Jesus Christ, accepting what He did for you on Calvary over 2000 years ago. You will never walk alone again. You will have a love, a kindness, and a support in your life that you have never known before. You will have the angels in heaven rejoicing, and you will acquire many brothers and sisters here on earth to pray for you and help you grow in your newfound life. Will the devil disappear forever now? Will you never have any more problems? Will your life be filled with only good fortune and joy? I wish that I could tell you yes. But the answer is no. You and everyone else will still be subject to this world and all the speed bumps that it will offer.

I say speed bumps because now what used to seem like mountains when you were facing them alone are only speed bumps when you turn them over to Christ. As you grow in your spiritual life, you will learn principles that will help you avoid most pitfalls you encounter as you go through life. That is why you must get a Bible. I would suggest a NKJV (New King James Version). This translation is the same as the New King James Version, but it is in plain everyday English and therefore much easier to read and understand. Get yourself into a good church. But I would caution you here that you always remember that you are serving Jesus Christ Himself and His Gospel of the Kingdom, and not any particular denomination. But the Bible does tell us to gather ourselves together for strength and support of one another. Never take your eyes off Jesus and you will be just fine. Get away from the people that you have been associating with in your life away from God. The enemy still dwells there and will make every attempt to regain you to his side. If you stumble and fall, get right back up, repent and return to the arms of Jesus. Do not get into the habit of "party hardy" on the weekend and returning to Christ on Monday morning. You only have power and protection over the devil when you are walking straight with Christ. Only the protection of the shed Blood of Jesus Christ can protect you from the evil one. Never fool yourself into thinking that you can defeat this monster alone. So my best advice to you is to avoid him at all costs and stay close to the One who proved His love for you by going to His death for you. No greater love has any man then when he gives up his life for another.

To get you started I have given you some Scriptures in the back of this book to read. Some of them are the Scriptures that I have paraphrased throughout this book. Others are encouraging Scriptures, and still others are promises of God for His chosen ones. And that, my dear friend, is you. God chose you from the foundations of time or you would not be giving your life to Him now. I know I was amazed to learn that when He saved my wretched soul from the very pits of hell.

God, like any good Father, will correct you from time to time. Suddenly things that you have always done and never given a second thought will start to bother you. Listen to it, because the Holy Spirit is correcting you. Have you ever started to do something kind of iffy and you got a really strong feeling that you should not do it? Well the Holy Spirit will instruct you this way, but even more strongly. Listen with your spiritual ears. Your spiritual hearing will get much better as you grow in the Lord. The Holy Spirit is the best friend you will ever have. In the physical, a true friend will always encourage you to do what is best for you and will keep you from getting into dark and troublesome places. In the spirit realm, the Holy Spirit will do this for you. He was sent here for this purpose. Although He will speak to you in spirit, He will keep you on the straight and narrow in the physical as well.

Jesus told many parables when He was on earth teaching His disciples. One of the parables was about how God, like a gardener, prunes the vines that do not bear fruit so that the whole tree may bear fruit. Likewise God will "prune" things from your life that are not good for you in order for you to grow and prosper as a whole in Him. All of the parables that Jesus used while teaching are amazing. Be sure to look for them and read them when you get your Bible.

There will be times when it will seem like God is on vacation. This means we are going through a trial. From now on, look at all trials as a potential for growth in your life. Even your earthly father will let go when you are taking your first bike ride without the training wheels. It is at times like these that the enemy will come in and try to remind you of your past again. You just say firmly, "Satan I rebuke you by the Blood of Jesus and get behind me." Never forget to say, "By the Blood of Jesus." You cannot come up against the devil alone, ever!

These times of silence were so very hard for me. It was scary, and I thought that I was going it alone. Once you learn to hear His voice, you know when it is not there. We love to have someone with us when we have to go through something hard. But then I heard a great woman of God, Paula White, state that "when the students are taking a test, the teacher never speaks." That was a breakthrough in my life! I was not alone. It was just a test. And I must have come far enough along in my walk with God for Him to test me. I now take pride in my tests and trials and consider them glory when I come out the other side. Just as your body needs workouts, your spirit man needs a personal trainer—and that is you. Once you have gone through a trial you will be amazed at the wisdom of God. And you will praise Him for your growth in Him. The next time another situation like this arises, you will soar like an eagle over the ordeal. Consider these times as "Spiritual Boot Camp." There is not any army in the world that enlists soldiers and then shakes their hands, pats them on the back, hands them a gun and sends them into battle expecting them to come out conquerors. Well, as you will discover in your new walk, you will be more that a conqueror in Christ. He will give you all the training and weapons you need to defeat your enemy. And you will want to go in and fight for the souls of your friends, family and loved ones by the time He is done with your training. You will find much of this training in a good church.

Never forget this one important thing: Your body is going to perish eventually. But the enemy wants every soul he can collect. Don't let yours be one of them. Fight the good fight for yourself and those you love.

Also remember to exercise your faith muscle every day. Remember that "faith is the substance of things hoped for and the evidence of things not seen." Faith comes from hearing the Word. Believe in God and read His manual for life (the Bible) every day. Whatever you do, don't give up when things get hard. Never forget that Jesus, as God made flesh, had a free will just like you do. If He had walked away from His great challenge, which is much greater than any challenge we will ever face, we would still not be able to have access to God the Father. Praise God that He stayed His course and was true to His challenge. Draw your strength in times of trial from His example. Even Jesus as He hung on the cross dying called out "Eli, Eli, lama sabachthani!" This meant *My God, My God, why hast thou forsaken me?* That was the "flesh" talking. The Spirit knows that God is there, and great will be our reward when our race is done. Jesus ran His race and now sits at the right hand of His Father God.

You don't have to wait for trials to obtain knowledge. Jesus told His disciples to ask and it would be given to them. If they would seek, they would find. If they knocked, the door would be opened. You will learn to wait on God and His wisdom even when you think that you have the solution. God's way is always better. Even if He okays your course of action, your confidence is higher when your plan has the blessing of the Father. Don't ever forget that every trial produces knowledge and that knowledge is your armor for another victory in Jesus.

And last, but not least, my dear abused ones, know that someone that does not even know you loves you and is praying for you every day until you come into your fullness in Christ. No matter how old, no matter how young, you can find your rest in Jesus, and He will set you free forever. Every one of you was created by our Heavenly Father. The enemy thinks that he has stolen your precious soul. Take it back right now. As long as you can draw your next breath, you can still do this. Know that your victory is in Jesus and through Him you will be a survivor and no longer the victim. The angels will rejoice in heaven and your name will be forever written in the Lamb's Book of Life. And when the Lord returns with a shout, you will recognize His voice and will eat from the Tree of Life forever. You will enter into the city and see the Bright and Morning Star, which is Jesus, and rule and reign with Him forever.

I said at the beginning of this book that it only took a sound, a song, a smell to bring back what has happened to us. But now I can tell you that the sound of Jesus' name and the songs of praise and worship that I now sing and hear bring back the memory of the best thing that ever happened in my life: the night that I gave my life to Jesus because I was forever set free. *And whom the Lord sets free is free indeed.* I thank Him for the encouragement and inspiration to write this book. All the glory is His.

Remember that I asked God why this happened to me, and I told you that He answered, "Because you were strong enough." Each one of us can use what has happened to us in one of two ways. We can let it destroy us, or we can destroy it. I was strong enough to survive, and so are you. You, too, have a story that God can use to touch and bring home others just like yourself. Share your story and your salvation for the glory of God. You are a hero. You are a survivor. You are not what your molester or abuser made you feel like. You have yet to see what God created you to be. Go with God and let him finish the work he started in you the day you were born. The Devil is a liar. Well, what are you waiting for? Go now and tell someone!

This is the single most important thing you will ever do in your life. You are about to turn your life, good, bad, and in between, over to Jesus. By His death and resurrection you were saved from eternal damnation, and by His stripes that He took on His back you were healed. Remember that you will now have access to all the power and gifts God has to offer. If you need encouragement or direction you can contact the author at EagleSpirit Ministries at www. eaglespiritministries.com.

PRAYER OF SALVATION

Dear Lord Jesus, I believe You are the Son of God. I believe You came to earth 2,000 years ago. I believe You died for me on the cross and shed Your blood for my salvation. I believe You rose from the dead and ascended on high. I believe and await Your return to rule and reign forever and ever, world without end. Dear Jesus, I come to You lost and a sinner. Forgive my sin. Cleanse me now with Your precious blood. Come into my heart and dwell forever. I receive You now as my Lord and Savior, and I long to serve and follow You all the days of my life from this day forward. From this moment on I belong to You and I leave the world and the enemy behind. I am born again. Amen

CONGRATULATIONS!!!! You are now a child of the living God, and you are entitled to *everything* that all the other children of God are entitled to. Don't you ever hang your head is shame again! Your sins have been washed away for all eternity by the Blood of Jesus. Get yourself to a Church, a Mission, or a Minister and get yourself a Bible. If you cannot afford one, they can direct you to where you can get one free. And remember, you have a new sister in Christ—me. I will be praying for you.

PUT ON YOUR ARMOR DAILY
(Don't leave home without it)
Taken from Ephesians 6:11-18

Help us this morning to put on the full armor of God so that we can take a stand against the devil's schemes. For our struggle is not against flesh and blood, but against the rulers, the authorities, and the powers of this dark world and against the spiritual forces of evil in the heavenly realms. Therefore we put on the full armor of God, so that when the day of evil comes, we may be able to stand our ground, and after we have done everything, to stand firm, with the belt of truth buckled around our waist, with the breastplate of righteousness in place, and with our feet fitted with the readiness that comes from the gospel of peace. In addition, may we take up the shield of faith, with which we can extinguish all the flaming arrows of the evil one. We take up the helmet of salvation and the sword of the Spirit, which is the word of God, and pray in the Spirit on all occasions in praise and glory to our Lord Jesus Christ, our Savior. Amen

The Our Father

Our Father who art in heaven, hallowed be Thy name. Thy Kingdom come, Thy will be done, on earth as it is in Heaven. Give us this day our daily bread, and forgive us our trespasses as we forgive those who trespass against us. And lead us not into temptation, but deliver us from evil, for Thine is the Kingdom and the Power and the Glory forever and ever. Amen

SCRIPTURE TO GET YOU STARTED
(All scripture is taken from the New International Version)

1 John: 1-9, The Word of Life: That which was from the beginning, which we have heard, which we have seen with our eyes, which we have looked at and our hands have touched, this we proclaim concerning the Word of life. The life appeared; we have seen it and testify to it, and we proclaim to you the eternal life, which was with the Father and has appeared to us. We proclaim to you what we have seen and heard, so that you also may have fellowship with us. And our fellowship is with the Father and with his Son, Jesus Christ. We write this to make our joy complete. This is the message we have heard from him and declare to you: God is light; in him there is no darkness at all. If we claim to have fellowship with him yet walk in the darkness, we lie and do not live by the truth. But if we walk in the light, as he is in the light, we have fellowship with one another, and the Blood of Jesus, his Son, purifies us from all sin. If we claim to be without sin, we deceive ourselves and the truth is not in us. If we confess our sins, he is faithful and just and will forgive us our sins and purify us from all unrighteousness. If we claim we have not sinned, we make him out to be a liar and his work has no place in our lives.

Forgive so that God will forgive you.

Matthew 6:14: Jesus says: For if you forgive men when they sin against you, your Heavenly Father will also forgive you. But if you do not forgive men their sins, your Father will not forgive your sins.

Share the news of your salvation.

Matthew 10: 32-33: Whoever acknowledges me before men, I will also acknowledge him before my Father in heaven. But whoever disowns me before men, I will disown him before my Father in heaven.

God will come through for you.

Matthew 7:7-11: Jesus says: Ask and it will be given to you, seek and you will find; knock and the door will be opened to you. For everyone who asks receives; he who seeks finds; and to him who knocks; the door will be opened. Which of you, if his son asks for bread, will give him a stone? Or if he asks for a fish, will give him a snake? If you, then, though you are evil, know how to give good gifts to your children, how much more will your Father in heaven give good gifts to those who ask him!

Come out from among them, and be considered sons and daughters of God.

2Corinthians 6: 17-18: Therefore come out from them and be separate, touch no unclean thing, and I will receive you. I will be a Father to you and you will be my sons and daughters, says the Lord Almighty.

What good does it do to gain everything and lose your soul?

Matthew 16: 26: Jesus says: What good will it be for a man if he gains the whole world, he loses his soul? Or what can a man give in exchange for his soul?

You will have peace beyond all understanding.

Matthew 11: 29: Jesus says: Come to me, all you who are weary and burdened and I will give you rest.

Philippians 4: 4-7: Rejoice in the Lord always. I will say it again; Rejoice! Let your gentleness be evident to all. The Lord is near. Do not be anxious about anything, but in everything, by prayer and petition, with thanksgiving, present your requests to God. And the peace of

God, which transcends all understanding, will guard your hearts and your minds in Christ Jesus.

Satan is real.

Job 1:6, Zechariah 3:2, Matthew 17:26, Matthew 16:23, Mark 4:15, Luke 10:18, and 22:3, Romans 16:20, 1 Corinthians 5:5, 2 Corinthians 11:14 and 12:7, 1 Titus 1:20, and Revelation 12: 9 and 20:2, and 20:7

Satan hates everyone.

1Peter 5:8: Be self controlled and alert. Your enemy the devil prowls around like a roaring lion looking for someone to devour. Resist him, standing firm in the faith, because you know that your brothers throughout the world are undergoing the same kind of sufferings.

The story of creation

Genesis 1:24-31, Genesis 2:1-22 and Genesis3:1-24

Satan disguises himself as a serpent.

Genesis 3:1

The damage done to humanity by Adam and Eve.

Genesis 3:1

To restore the covenant God clothed them in skins (not fig leaves).

Genesis 3:21

Satan only comes to steal and kill and destroy, but Jesus came so you might have life and have it more abundantly.

John 10:10: Jesus says: The thief (Satan) comes only to steal and kill and destroy; I have come that they may have life, and have it to the full.

Jesus will ask the Father to send the Comforter (the Holy Spirit).

John 14:16-17: Jesus says: And I will ask the Father, and he will give you another Counselor to be with you forever, the Spirit of truth. The world cannot accept hi, because it neither sees him nor knows him. But you know him because he lives with you and will be in you.

No greater love has any man.

John 15:13: Jesus says: Greater love has no one than this that he lay down his life for his friends.

God chose you.

John 15:16: Jesus says: You did not choose me but I chose you and appointed you to go and bear fruit, fruit that will last.

God will prune you to improve you.

John 15:1-2: Jesus says: I am the true vine, and my Father is the gardener. He cuts off every branch in me that bears no fruit, while every branch that does bear fruit he prunes so that it will be even more fruitful.

God will never leave you or abandon you.

Hebrews 13:5-6: Keep your lives free from the love of money and be content with what you have, because God has said, "Never will I leave you; never will I forsake you." So we say with confidence, "The Lord is my helper; I will not be afraid. What can man do to me?"

Your name will be written in the Lamb's Book of Life.

Revelation 21:26-28: The glory and honor of the nations will be brought into it. Nothing impure will ever enter it, nor will anyone who does what is shameful or deceitful, but only those whose names are written in the Lamb's Book of life.

Revelation 22:14-16: Jesus says: Blessed are those who wash their robes, that they may have the right to the tree of life and may go through the gates into the city. Outside are the dogs, those who practice magic arts, the sexually immoral, the murderers, the idolaters and everyone who loves and practices falsehood. I, Jesus, have sent my angel to give you this testimony for the churches. I am the Root and the Offspring of David, and the bright Morning Star.